John A. Smith

Uncle John upon His Travels

Letters from Europe to the Children

John A. Smith

Uncle John upon His Travels
Letters from Europe to the Children

ISBN/EAN: 9783337209438

Printed in Europe, USA, Canada, Australia, Japan

Cover: Foto ©Andreas Hilbeck / pixelio.de

More available books at **www.hansebooks.com**

𝔏etters from 𝔈urope to the 𝔈hildren.

UNCLE JOHN

UPON HIS TRAVELS.

Compiled for Publication, with an Introduction,

BY AUNT ESTHER.

ILLUSTRATED.

CHICAGO:
THE LAKESIDE PUBLISHING COMPANY.
1870.

Entered according to act of Congress in the year 1870, by
THE LAKESIDE PUBLISHING COMPANY,
In the office of the Librarian of Congress, at Washington.

CONTENTS.

LETTER FIRST.
Life on Shipboard, - - - - - - - 11

LETTER SECOND.
Life on Shipboard.—Concluded, - - - - 23

LETTER THIRD.
A London Sunday-school, - - - - - - 32

LETTER FOURTH.
Crossing Mountains, - - - - - - - 47

LETTER FIFTH.
The Two Cemeteries, - - - - - - - 60

LETTER SIXTH.
Christmas in Paris, - - - - - - - 74

LETTER SEVENTH.
The Story of a King, - - - - - - - 87

LETTER EIGHTH.
The Story of a King.—Concluded, - - - 98

LETTER NINTH.
The Birds in the Palace Garden, - - - - 108

LETTER TENTH.
The Birds in the Palace Garden.—Concluded, - 117

LETTER ELEVENTH.
The Old Soldiers and their General, - - - 125

INTRODUCTION.

In another part of the book you will find a picture of the Palace and a portion of the Garden, in which you may perceive the place where we sat. On the right of the picture you will see a fine statue; close to this there are chairs for persons walking in the Gardens who may choose to occupy them We took possession of two chairs close to the statue, and once more witnessed the feeding of the birds, as mentioned in the Letter. Our Heavenly Father's care of the birds encouraged us to trust him anew, for we felt sure that we were of more value to him than many sparrows.

Returning home, Uncle John was very tired, and went to rest in his accustomed place. After a little time he requested me to bolster him in the bed, and give him pencil and paper, which I did. The Letter entitled "The Birds in the Palace Garden" was the result.

"The Story of a King" comes to my mind as I gaze upon the picture of the Place de la Concorde. There are two fine fountains, each having twelve statues, every one of which holds a fish in its hands from whose mouth pours the water thrown up into the basin above. Between these fountains you will see a tall column which is called an obelisk. It was brought from Thebes, and placed where it now stands in the reign of Louis Philippe. Upon the spot where you see this obelisk stood the scaffold on which Lous XVI. was beheaded, as described in the "Story of a King." About twenty paces from it, toward the right of the picture, and near the Tuileries gate, his beautiful queen, Marie Antoinette, suffered a like bloody death. If the men who did these cruel things had been taught from the Bible in their childhood to "fear God" and "honor the King," they would not, I am certain, have stained their hands thus with the blood of those whom they had so many reasons to love and reverence.

There is another picture which I must tell you about. In the "Story of a Castle," Little Jane, "The Young Cottager," is mentioned. She is here seen learning the verses on the tombstones. Her companions are with her, and Legh Richmond, the pastor, is instructing other children near the church. It is more than seventy years since what this picture represents took place, and this Saturday afternoon school for religious instruction, for there were no Sunday-schools then, has been heard of throughout the world by reason of the conversion of Little Jane. She died at the age of fifteen.

I must tell you the conversation with her pastor that led him to think her a child of God. She was upon a sick-bed, and had sent for him to instruct and comfort her. She had learned two lines from a tombstone near that which you see her studying. They are these —

> "Hail, glorious gospel, heavenly light, whereby
> We live with comfort and with comfort die."

At one time during her illness she quoted these lines to Mr. Richmond, and then said, "I wished that glorious gospel was mine, that I might live and die with comfort, and it seemed as if I thought it would be so. I never felt so happy in all my life before. The words were often in my thoughts,

> 'Live with comfort and with comfort die.'

"Glorious gospel, indeed, I thought."

"My dear child," said Mr. Richmond, "what is the meaning of the word gospel?"

"Good news."

"Good news for whom?"

"For wicked sinners, sir."

"Who sends this good news for wicked sinners?"

"The Lord Almighty."

"And who brings this good news?"

"Sir, *you* brought it to *me*."

"Here," says Mr. Richmond, "my soul melted in an instant, and I could not repress the tears which the emotion excited."

I heard from a lady who keeps the key of the cemetery, that travelers are often there to look upon her grave. It is like other graves of poor children, only with a beautiful white stone, always kept clean and legible by those who honor her memory. Thus is the Scripture verified, "Them that honor me I will honor."

This, you see, is not a story book, although there are stories in it. But they are true stories. Uncle John and I are both perfectly certain that children can be interested in things true, and which are intended to instruct as well as to entertain. May you find in this little book both pleasure and profit, is the wish of

AUNT ESTHER.

Uncle John upon his Travels.

Letter First.

LIFE ON SHIPBOARD.

Dear Boys and Girls:

WHEN I was a child, there was a queer little verse which we were very fond of repeating, although I always wondered, and have not done wondering yet, what it could mean. This is the way it ran:

> "Uncle John is very sick;
>   What shall we send him?
> A piece of pie, a piece of cake.
>   What shall we send it in?
> In a golden saucer."

I little thought that one day I should be, myself, Uncle John, and that while tossing and rolling in a ship at sea this funny little verse — at least its first line — would be almost the only thing I could think of. The things, however, which it is proposed to "send" Uncle John were of very little value to me. I would not have given a pin for all the "pies and cakes" on the ship, nor for as many "golden saucers" as could be piled to the top of the mast. One day the stewardess, kind Mrs. Travers, asked me, "Is there not something you would like to have?" and I answered her, "I believe that the best thing in all the world for me, just now, would be a good slice of solid ground." I must tell you what a kind friend I found in the man who takes care of the state-rooms. They call him the bed-room steward. His name is Frank Moffat. He was as kind to me as possible; brought me the things I wanted with such a pleasant smile, and would come and ask me so nicely what I preferred to eat, suggesting such little messes as he knew are best when one is sea-sick, that really it seemed as if he thought I was Uncle John, and that all the boys and girls wished him to take good care of me. I shall never forget Frank Moffat, and I hope that you will not, either.

After all, I am not sorry that I was sick, it seems so delicious to be well again. Indeed, I think that very often, perhaps generally, when people are getting well they are glad they have been sick. *Getting well* is almost better than health itself, while I am sure that we appreciate health after sickness as we never did before. I wonder if when we reach heaven — as I earnestly pray we all of us may, in God's good time — we shall not be all the happier for having suffered so much on the earth; if even the holiness of heaven will not be brighter and more blessed to us after having seen and felt the hatefulness and the wretchedness of sin.

I did not think, at one time, that I should make my first letter to you about our passage across the Atlantic, but wait until I had met with something in England, where I now am, that might interest you. You see, however, that I am in a hurry to be talking to you again, and you have made me believe that you yourselves will be in some haste to hear from us. Besides, I suppose that very few of you have ever seen a ship, and none of you perhaps understand very well what a ship is, or how they live and what they do on board of one. So I am going to tell you, and I think we shall find a nice little Sunday-school lesson in it all.

The name of our ship is "The Nevada." You see that she has the name of that little State away over among the Rocky Mountains, in America; how very far away it seems to me, now! She is a magnificently large ship; I scarcely can tell you, so that you can understand, how large. I suppose that if she were placed along the north side of the Court-House Square, in Chicago, she would reach at least two-thirds of the way from Clark Street to LaSalle, and I am certain that she is as long as almost any of the squares, or blocks, in your smaller towns or cities. Being a steamship, she has a very powerful engine nearly midway from one end to the other. One way from it, towards the stern, is a mast, and the other way from it, towards the bow, is another. Each of these has four sails, some of them quite large. There is also a sail reaching from the middle of the fore-mast to the bow. Thus there are nine in all, and when they are all set, and the wind blows fair, you may be sure that, what with the sails and what with the steam, the good ship flies like a bird.

There are a good many officers and men on such a ship as the "Nevada." Besides the Captain, there is the first officer, the second officer, the third officer, the purser, and some others whose titles I do not know. These are all skillful men; but the one I noticed as much as any other was one whom I have not named yet — the boatswain. He is emphatically the man of all work. He seems to be the connecting link between the officers and the crew, as he belongs to both. He commands like an officer, but he works like every other sailor. It is his business to see that what the other officers command is done, and often, in order to make the men work right and with a will, he takes hold and shows them how. If the sails are to be set or taken in, he tells them what ropes to pull, and sometimes lays hold and pulls with them; if the deck is to be scoured, he tells the men to do it, and if they don't suit him in their way of doing it, he goes at it himself; if a sail is to be mended, you may see him showing how to do it, or perhaps even doing it. He has a silver whistle hung by a cord about his neck, and often you would hear that whistle sounding through the ship, so shrill that it seemed to cut the air like a knife. While the men drew up the sails, for example, he would blow upon his whistle, giving them the signal; in one way of blowing it that they should pull, pull harder, harder yet, and in another that the sail was up and they might stop. When the men were in their cabin, he would blow his whistle, and out they would come. A wonderful thing, when you think of it, is the boatswain's silver whistle. Our boatswain was a short, thick-set man, not nicely dressed like the other officers, but looking as if all he thought about was getting the work of the ship done. He had a sharp, black eye, and a rugged face, which had a look all the while as if he were saying to himself, "What lazy dogs these men are!" He was not a polite man, by a great deal, and seemed to have but very few words for any body, even his superior officers. His voice was hoarse and rugged, like himself, as if it might have become so by his swallowing so much north wind. I don't know his name, but if

I were to give him one, it would be Jack Rough-and-Ready. I liked him, for my part, about as well as any man on the ship, he seemed so thorough-going and so sturdy.

Now I must tell you a few things about what they do on a ship. A curious part of it is the way they have of dividing the time. They have clocks and watches to be sure, but for certain purposes they have bells. There are two bells on the ship, one near the stern where the man is who steers, and another forward of the engine. These bells are rung, one after another, at each hour and half hour. For example, in this way: Say they begin to reckon their time at twelve o'clock, noon. At half-past twelve each bell is struck once. At one o'clock each is struck twice, or with one quick double stroke. This is *two bells*. At half-past one this double stroke is repeated, and followed by one single stroke. At two they give each bell two double strokes; this is *four bells*. At half-past two the same, with the single stroke as before, for the half. At three, there are three double strokes, making *six bells*, and at half-past the same as before. At four there are four double strokes, and this is *eight bells*. And now they begin again and go the same round; so that five o'clock is two bells, six o'clock is four bells, seven o'clock is six bells, eight o'clock is eight bells. Then nine o'clock is two bells again, ten o'clock is four bells, eleven o'clock is six bells, and twelve o'clock is eight bells.

Thus you see that *eight bells* comes three times in every twelve hours, with intervals of four hours each between. At each of these eight bells some important things are done, such as permitting those who have had charge of the vessel during the four hours to rest, and calling others to take their places; that is changing the watch. So these intervals are called *watches*. In ancient times they had similar things, not only on ship-board, but in armies and camps, and so common was this that even other people besides soldiers and sailors would divide the night, especially, in the same way. Don't you remember some places in the New Testament where it speaks about the third and fourth "watches" of the night?

Another thing I must tell you about is how they ascertain how fast the ship goes, and how far she sails each day. Of course, it is not, when you are on a ship at sea, as when you are riding in a railway train on land. There are no milestones to show you how far you have gone, and how much farther you have to go. At the same time it is quite as important for those in charge of a ship to know where they are, as it is for those in charge of a train. Now they tell how fast a ship goes by what is called *casting the log*. I can remember when I thought that really they did find this out by throwing a log into the sea, but how that would show it puzzled me, as I think it would almost anybody.

But the log, it so happens, is just no log at all. It is a long cord, about as large round as a clothes-line, fastened at one end to a kind of reel, or large spool, on which it is wound. This big spool has a smooth round stick running through it lengthwise, about which it turns easily, and each end of this, when the log is in use, is held by a sailor. At the other end of the line, that which is dropped into the sea, is a small cloth bag, perhaps six inches long and four inches broad, with one end open and the other shut. They "cast the log" by dropping this end of the line and its little bag into the sea, with the open end of the bag towards the ship. Of course the bag fills with water, and then begins to drag, being heavier than it was before. It drags just hard enough to make the big spool turn round and the line run off, while it remains very nearly in the same place itself. Now, as it is the motion of the ship that makes the line run off, of course the line goes out just as fast as the ship moves, and if you know how many feet of line have run out in a given time, you know how many feet the ship has gone in the same time. They have a way of knowing this.

One of the sailors, while the rest are managing the line, holds in his hand a glass, made like an hour-glass, but so arranged that the sand in it runs from one of the broad ends into the other, through the little passage in the middle, in a much less time than one hour. We will say that it is half a minute, or fifteen seconds. There are knots made in the line at certain distances; suppose it to be twenty-two feet. Two hundred and forty of these knots, with the twenty-two feet between each of them, would make just a mile, or 5,280 feet. Two hundred and forty times fifteen seconds, too, is 3,600 seconds, or the number of seconds in an hour. So fifteen seconds is the same part of an hour that twenty-two feet is of a mile. Thus, you see, if the ship went only fast enough so that one of these knots would run off — one of these spaces of twenty-two feet — in fifteen seconds, it would be going at the rate of just one mile an hour. The sailor would call that one "knot" an hour, because only one knot of the line had run out. That would be very slow sailing indeed. But suppose twelve of the knots run off in fifteen seconds, — you come along then and you notice that Jack's face looks very bright, and you ask him, "How does she go now?" and he says, "Twelve knots, sir." He means that the ship is going at the rate of twelve miles in an hour; and his face looks bright because the sailors all like to have the ship go fast.

Now, you see that by casting the log several times, and comparing the results, they can in any case know what is the average rate of sailing. These several results, with the sum of them for each day, they put down in what is called the "log-book." I will tell you what our log-book showed as to our rate of sailing: On the first day we sailed 237 miles, on the second 265, on the third 270, on the fourth 281, on the fifth 274, on the sixth 270, on the seventh 292, on the eighth 284, on the ninth 300, on the tenth 315, on the eleventh 240. The sum of all these numbers is 3,028. The distance from New York to Liverpool is, I believe, about that. So you see that they can know pretty nearly how fast a ship sails every day.

There will be something more to tell you in the next letter.

LETTER SECOND.

LIFE ON SHIPBOARD — CONCLUDED.

Dear Boys and Girls:

STILL another thing it is very important to know, and that is whereabouts on the ocean the ship is; that is, its latitude and longitude. I will try to tell you how they find this, and in as few words as possible. Some of you know already, that if a person is standing somewhere in that part of the earth where the equator is — that is the line that is supposed to run round it from east to west — he will see the sun at noon directly over his head. If he then walks away from that place and comes north a few miles, he will see the sun, as he looks up to it at noon, not exactly overhead, but a little to the south of him, as if the sun had moved, and not he. And the sun *seems* to move just as fast in one direction as he *does* move in the other. Suppose, then, that he wants to know how far north he has come. If he can find how far the sun has seemed to move south, that will tell him, and that will be his *latitude*, that is, it will show him how far he is from the equator. Now the Captain of a ship has an instrument which he calls a quadrant — a very curious one, but I must not describe it — by means of which he can always tell, when the sun is in sight, how far the sun is from the point in the sky directly overhead. We will suppose that our Captain some day finds, after taking an "observation," as they call it, that the sun is fifty degrees down from that point towards the place where the sea and sky seem to meet, or the horizon. He knows, then, that his ship is at the fiftieth degree of north latitude. That is, he is fifty degrees north of the equator; that is where he is, reckoning north and south.

How can he tell where he is, reckoning east and west? You know that every circle has three hundred and sixty degrees. The sun, every day, in consequence of the earth turning fairly over just once in that time, *seems*, itself, to have gone round the earth in a circle. Of course, in that circle there are 360 degrees. It takes it 24 hours to go through that number of degrees. Divide 360 by 24 and it will show you how many degrees it passes over each hour. You will find that it is just fifteen. Now, the earth revolving from west to east, the sun seems to move, in consequence, from east to west, and this it is that makes the *time of day*, as you know; and in making the time of day it goes, as I showed you, just fifteen degrees of distance in one hour of time.

Let us now imagine two men standing, one towards the east and the other towards the west, and in a straight line, from one to the other. The one at the west calls out:

"Halloo, over there, my friend, you early bird, always farther along in the day than I am, let me try how I may. Do you know how far apart we are?"

"Why, no," says Early Bird, "I declare I do not; but I think it must be a good piece, a thousand miles or so, for I can hardly hear you call."

"Well, then," says the other, "tell me, at any rate, what time it is by your watch. The sun always reaches you before it does me, and they taught me, when I was a boy, that he goes round the world at the rate of fifteen degrees, or nine hundred miles, as there are sixty miles in a degree, in an hour. So, if we compare our watches, and see what the difference in time is, I guess we can tell what the difference in *place*, or the distance, is." You see that as he is towards the West he is a Yankee, and so he says "*I guess.*"

Early Bird looks at his watch, and it is just two o'clock. Yankee looks at his, and it is exactly one o'clock. "Just an hour's difference," calls out Yankee, "and so the distance is fifteen degrees, or nine hundred miles."

"Well," says Early Bird, "I thought it must be not far from a thousand miles, your voice sounded so faint. You know men can't talk to each other at a distance of much more than a thousand miles apart."

So you see there is always a difference of

fifteen degrees in distance, east and west, between places for every hour's difference in time, as shown by the sun. Now, if there should be some one place on the earth's surface agreed upon from which distance should be reckoned, and if a person sailing on the ocean could know, at any time of day, exactly what time it was at that place, he could tell his distance from it. The captain of a ship *has* something that tells him this, exactly. It is called a chronometer, and it shows, always, what time it is in London, the place from which distance east and west is usually reckoned. Suppose, then, that one day our Captain looks at his chronometer and finds that in London it is just eleven o'clock. Then he says, "If I can find out what time it is here, I shall know where I am, and I shall know this," he adds, "if I can find how high the sun is." So he takes his quadrant, as before, and measures by it, not this time how *low down* the sun is, but how *high up* it is. He finds that where his ship now is it is ten o'clock. There is, therefore, a difference of one hour of time, and so his distance from London is fifteen degrees, or nine hundred miles. In other words, his longitude, or distance west from London, is fifteen degrees. Thus he has ascertained that his distance north is fifteen degrees, and his distance west fifteen degrees. He finds the place on the map where these lines of latitude and longitude meet, and that shows him just where he is.

I ought to add that the Captain's map, or chart, shows him always where he *ought* to be. If, then, he finds that in this case he is where he ought *not* to be, he goes to his compass, and directs the course to be changed; that is, commands the man at the wheel, or helm, to turn it, so that the ship will move in the way it ought to go.

There are other things which I might tell you, but this must suffice now, and I am afraid I have been too long already. But, dear boys and girls, what may it all remind us of? Suppose we say it reminds us of the ship "Salvation." In this ship Jesus is the Captain; and the wonderful thing about him is that he is not sometimes on deck and sometimes in the cabin, sometimes in the forward part of the ship, sometimes in the after-part, sometimes awake, and sometimes asleep. He is at each moment in every part of the ship alike. His " eyes are in every place, beholding the evil and the good." The officers in this ship of which Jesus is the captain, are his ministers; but they are not, as officers frequently do, to think themselves better than the rest. They must be more like the boatswain, " ready to every good word and work," than like the first, second, and third officers, who walk the deck in gentlemen's clothes. Then again, in the ship which Jesus commands there are no passengers, or at least there *ought* to be none; no one whose business it simply is to enjoy himself, be waited upon, walk about the deck, eat, drink, and sleep; all must *help work the ship*. The compass is God's word, and it always points straight to heaven. Casting the log is examining ourselves, whether we be in the faith. Taking observations is studying the history of God's dealings, whether with us, or with the church at large; with his gracious, unchanging purpose as the sun by day and the star by night. How happy, if we all sail in this good ship, " looking unto Jesus," our Captain, "the author and the finisher of our faith!" How happy if, on a much fairer morning than that on which our ship sailed into Liverpool, you and I, dear young reader, sail into the heavenly port, safely arrived from the long voyage!

I must tell you in a word about the children on board. There were seven of them. They gave me their names, and I have them down in my note-book. They took a great liking to Aunt Esther, at which I am not the least surprised—are you? One evening they made her tell them a story for every letter in the alphabet. After she had got through she came into the state-room where Uncle John was and said, "Oh dear!" and when she told me what she had been doing, I am sure I did not wonder she should say, "Oh dear!"

But now, Good-bye. I am like all other talkative old men; I never know when to leave off. It is as when we were at the harbor of Queenstown, in Ireland, and the pilot wanted them to stop the ship. "Stop her," he called out, but they did not seem to understand. "*Stop her!*" he vociferated once more, with all his strength.

The reader of this description, I am sure, has been saying, for some time, "Stop her;" and now he says, "*Stop her!*" Well, I *will* stop her. And now she stops.

UNCLE JOHN.

LETTER THIRD.

A LONDON SUNDAY-SCHOOL.

Dear Boys and Girls:

AM very glad that I am able to describe to you, in this letter, a London Sunday-school, and to tell you something about the Sunday-schools generally of this great city. Last Sabbath, in the afternoon, I went with Col. J. T. Griffin, who once lived in Chicago, and was Superintendent of the North Baptist School, to the Sunday-school of Regent's Park chapel, where Rev. Wm. Landels, D.D., a very able and excellent man, is pastor. You see that I say "chapel," and not "church," as we should say in America. To "attend church," in this country, is to go to some of the places of worship of the Church of England, that is the church

supported by the Government, the Established Church. This is a way of speaking which people have, although Baptists, Methodists, and other bodies, think that their churches *are* churches, just as much as those connected with the Establishment. There is a church at Regent's Park chapel, and it is a Baptist church, and a good one too. I will tell you more about the Sunday-school further on. Just here I must deliver a message from the children, and in order to come at it easily, perhaps I had best tell how they came to send it.

Uncle John was invited to address the school, but at first declined because he thought everything would be so strange to him that he should be embarrassed, and frightened, and not know what to say. But as he went round among the classes he found that the boys and girls looked just as boys and girls do in America, and they were so pleasant, and seemed so much interested in trying to learn good things out of the Bible, that finally he concluded he should not be so much afraid of them, after all. And then, as he told them in a little speech which he made, he wished to write to his young friends in America about this, the first Sunday-school which he had visited in London, and it did not seem quite fair to do this without asking their consent. So he said to them,

"Are you willing that I should write about you to the boys and girls of the Northwestern S ates in America? If so, just raise your right hands, that I may know."

And every hand came up; they seemed very willing, and very much pleased.

Then he said: "Now the Sunday-school children in America will, I am sure, be greatly interested in learning about this school in London, that wonderful city of which they have heard so much. If they had known that I was going to meet you here, they would all have sent their love to you. Would you not like to send this message to them? Shall I say to them that the boys and girls in the Regent's Park Sunday-school in London, send their love to the Sunday-schools in the Northwestern States of America?"

And every hand came up again. This is how it happened that I have this message to send you. Of course, they did not know that I was

Uncle John until I told them, nor did they realize that Sunday-school children in England could love Sunday-school children in America, and send pleasant messages to them, until they had been reminded of it; but then they found that they could. And this led Uncle John to mention another thing which he will repeat here, because he would like to have his own boys and girls think about it. He said:

"It seems almost singular that we should be able to love persons whom we have never seen, and yet I am sure that we can. The children of America can love the children of England, and those in England can love those in America, although they should never see each other in this world. Can any of you tell me of some one whom none of us have ever seen, yet whom we all ought to love?"

A little boy answered very promptly, "Jesus!"

"Yes, Jesus; we all ought to love him though we have never seen him, and many of us, I hope, do so. But we do not love him all at once, nor just so soon as we begin hearing or reading about him. What must we first become, that we may love Jesus as we ought?"

The answer was, very promptly again, "Christians."

This was a right answer, and Uncle John told them he hoped they might all become Christians, and might all love Jesus, even now while they cannot see him, that at last they may rejoice the more, when they *shall* "see him as he is."

This nice and pleasant school at Regent's Park has upon its list of scholars 756 names; the average attendance is 513. There is, besides, a branch school, what we should call a mission school, with an average attendance of 240. In the two schools there are just about one thousand scholars, all told; which is certainly a very good number indeed. Some things about "the home school," or the one at the chapel, are different from what is customary in America. There are *three* departments in it, instead of two, as with us. These are called the "Senior School," the "Junior School," and the "Infant School." They meet in separate rooms, but rooms that open into each other in a very convenient way. In the senior school are the largest scholars, in the junior school those younger, and in the infant school the little bits of folks. I visited all three, and was delighted to see how orderly, attentive, and earnest they seemed to be, with very few exceptions.

Another thing which they have, and we do not, is the Sunday-morning service. It is the custom in London for the schools to meet twice on each Lord's day; in the morning at ten o'clock, and in the afternoon at three. I find, upon inquiry, that the afternoon school is always much better attended than the morning one, by both scholars and teachers. Indeed, I think a good many are beginning to doubt if they can keep up the morning school at all. Now, at the Regent's Park chapel, the Sunday-school workers, some months ago, began to ask themselves if they could not find some way to make the morning session more attractive to the children. So they determined that they would have what they call a "Sunday-morning service"—not lessons, as in the afternoon, but what we Americans term "a good time generally," in singing, prayers, and addresses. They find that the plan works very well indeed. The children like it, the teachers like it, and they have no difficulty now in securing a full attendance. They meet at ten o'clock, spend about half the time till half-past eleven in singing and praying, and the remainder in addresses.

I will tell you something more about these addresses. They are given, mostly, by those connected with the school as officers and teachers, and other members of the church. If I give you some of the subjects you will see a little what they are. On the first Sabbath in October, for example, Col. Griffin, who is a greatly beloved member of the church, and has an exceedingly interesting Bible class in the afternoon, addressed the children at their morning service upon the word "Up." On the first Sabbath in the present month (November) he addressed them upon the letters "H. H. H."— by which he meant the words, "Hark, Heed, Hold." On the first Sabbath in December his subject will be "Rest." Mr. S. Shirley, a former superintendent, who was very kind in showing Uncle John the different rooms, is to give the address upon the third Sabbath in December. His subject will be, " A Little

Child." I think I know *what* little child he will talk about. Mr. Holman, the present superintendent, speaks at these services quite frequently. One of his subjects has been, "Making a Curtsey," another, "Fallen Leaves," another, "A Story of a November Fog." Next month he is to speak upon "A Burning Village." Other subjects have been, "A Bunch of Keys," Mr. Brady; "Links in a Chain," Mr. Bailey; "Lessons from the Life of Moses," Mr. Cluck; "Snakes," Mr. Bompar; "House-Building," Mr. Cluck. These are just specimens. You see that they are what the grown people sometimes call "suggestive;" that is, they are things that make us think, almost whether we will or no.

I asked some of the brethren if this Sunday morning service did not interfere with that of the congregation up stairs. They said it did not, for the children meet half an hour before the congregation does, and so get all through with their singing before the up-stairs' service begins, and after that are very quiet. They are dismissed at half-past eleven, and are gone home before the congregation to whom the pastor has been preaching begins to come out. It seemed to me, however, that I should myself prefer to have the children of the families in the congregation sit with their parents, at the regular service; but I was told that very few of these children in the Sunday-school are children in families of the congregation. They are mostly of families who perhaps do not attend service regularly anywhere, and many of them, I presume, would be running in the streets if this provision were not made for them. With us, you know, the Sunday-schools are made up very largely from the families of the church and the congregation. I do not think that in America we need such an arrangement so much as it is needed here, and perhaps could not make it work well, anyhow. But I could not help feeling sorry that the children of the regular congregation did not attend the schools here more than they do, both for their own sake and for that of the wandering children whom they might influence by such a good example.

They are very active, and very systematic, I should think, in this Regent's Park school.

They have the work of each three months laid out in advance, and printed upon cards. Thus on one of the cards I found this:

Thursday, Nov. 4.—Old Scholars' Meeting. Tea at 7 o'clock,
Tuesday, Nov. 9.—Scholars' Missionary Working Party at 3 o'clock.
Tuesday, Nov. 16.—Scholars' Missionary Meeting, with Addresses.
Tuesday, Nov. 23.—Teachers' Business Meeting. Chair to be taken at 3 o'clock.

On another card, which is intended to be given to each teacher at the beginning of the month, there is stated what particular service each one is to perform on each Sabbath of the month. Perhaps it is " sit with the children; " perhaps " attend at quarter to three," for singing or some other purpose, I suppose; perhaps " open " or " close the Senior School," with prayer; perhaps " open " or " close the Junior School." Then, under this, I find the following:

"*It is essential, in order to secure efficient teaching and good order, for each Teacher—*
1. To prepare the lessons before entering the class.

2. To attend early, and in case of absence to furnish a substitute.

3. To visit scholars at their homes.

4. To punctually fulfill school engagements; and

5. To insist upon silence immediately the Superintendent strikes the bell."

They are doing a good deal of work, evidently, in the Regent's Park church and school. Just see how many societies they have. There is the "Domestic Mission Society," which raised, last year, about fifteen hundred dollars. The branch, or mission school, is sustained by this society; it provides preaching, also, in some of the destitute parts of the city; it has a "Mother's Class," a "Medical Friends' Club," a "Mutual Aid Society," a "Loan Library," and a "Penny Bank," by means of which poor persons are enabled to save a little money. There is besides a Young Men's Association, which has lectures, holds meetings for discussions and devotional purposes, and a Sunday conversation meeting, or Bible class, of which I spoke before, and over which Col. Griffin presides. This meeting, or class, is held every Sunday afternoon, and is made up of all who can be induced to attend it. The young men and young ladies of the church and school go out upon the street half an hour before the time, with tracts, and invite, "compel," all they can to "come in;" and a good many come. Sometimes there are as many as a hundred present. Conversions, too, frequently occur; and there have been instances of careless ones, brought in from the street, convicted of sin at their first meeting with the class, and soon after brought to Christ. What a truly blessed thing this is!

Besides these organizations already named, there are the "Benevolent Society," whose object is to visit and relieve cases of sickness and extreme necessity among the poor, at their own habitations;" the "Dorcas Society," which purchases and makes up clothing for poor women in the neighborhood; and the "Missionary Society" which raises money for foreign missions. As nearly as I can ascertain, these several organizations, including the Sunday-schools, raise for the purposes named, at least $4,500.

I have given you all these particulars that you and the teachers in Sunday-schools, and the members of churches, so far as such may care to read what I write, may see something of the way London Baptists work. Probably other churches are equally systematic and faithful. I do not wonder that the Lord blesses them.

I must now tell you that there is in London a Sunday-school Union, in which the faithful workers in different denominations are united for promoting the good cause. Some of the gentlemen connected with this society, especially Mr. Fountain J. Hartley, have been very obliging to me in furnishing me the means of information regarding this work. I wish I had more room than I have to tell you about it. The exact number of teachers and scholars connected with all the schools of London I have not been able to ascertain, as not all the schools of the city are represented in the Union. As nearly as can be ascertained, however, there were in 1867, three years ago, about 986 schools in the city — almost a thousand — with 216,151 scholars in them. I presume there must be now over a thousand schools, with perhaps nearly or quite a quarter of a million of scholars. Of schools connected with the Union there were, in 1866, or three years since, 652, with 160,158 scholars. Of the schools 524 have libraries, containing in all 147,284 volumes; 128 of the schools, however, have no libraries. It was supposed, at the time just mentioned, that there were, in England and Wales, 3,000,000 of scholars, and probably this is not far from the number now.

London contains, you know, a population of more than three millions. It is a pleasing fact that there should be nearly a quarter of a million of Sunday-scholars in the number. But there are a great many boys and girls, even now, who know nothing about Sunday-schools or about Jesus. Faithful men and women are trying hard to provide for them and bring them where they may learn how to be saved. But it is a vast work. Think, dear children, of a single city with more people in it than the whole State of Illinois! O, how many poor and suffering ones there are here! My heart aches for them, as I meet them every time I go out upon the street. If Uncle John had his pockets full of money when he takes his hat and cane and goes for a walk, he might come back without a sixpence, if he was to give to all who ask, and to whom he would be glad to give. But he has to remember that there is both a "Number One" and a "Number Two" for him to think of, and it would not answer for him to have no money left for the landlady who keeps the lodging-house, or to buy railroad tickets when he starts next Monday or Tuesday morning for Paris. So you see he must try to harden his head, if not his heart, and not be *too* "soft."

UNCLE JOHN.

LETTER FOURTH.

CROSSING MOUNTAINS.

Dear Boys and Girls:

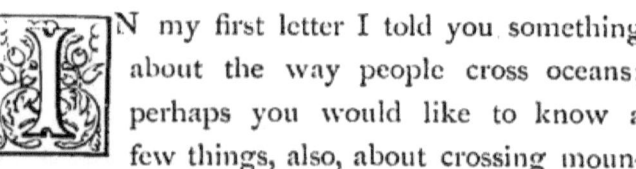N my first letter I told you something about the way people cross oceans; perhaps you would like to know a few things, also, about crossing mountains. There is a considerable difference between the two undertakings, yet sometimes people have to do about as queer things in the one as they do in the other.

When, in America, I was thinking and planning about this visit to Europe, it seemed to me that it would be quite an easy matter to get from London to Rome. The whole of Europe takes up but a small part of the map of the eastern continent, and although I knew, of course, that there are some big countries and big people in it, still I somehow imagined that one could run across it, from north to south at all events, very much as he might take a run from Chicago down to Cairo. Uncle John, in his simplicity— and all old men who have scarcely been out of sight of their own chimney-tops are simple— did not realize that it is almost fifteen hundred miles from London to Rome, and that whoever goes from one to the other, be it winter, be it summer, must either cross the Alps, or must take a ride on the Mediterranean— a sea that is always, or at least very often, out of temper in the winter season— or must go a roundabout way in the stage.

When I reached Paris, I found that either I must take to the sea again, and suffer probably as I had already done, or the mountains must be crossed. They told us of a gentleman who had but a few days before been stopped by the snow at the top of Mont Cenis, where the railway over the Alps is, and had spent four days, "living on dry bread and black coffee." Still I must go to Rome, and I was less afraid of the snow than of the sea-sickness; so my friend, Mr. "Keynote," and I said to each other. "One man has been snowed in and had a tough time. Others are crossing every day without getting snowed in. Evidently it can be done, so let us try." And that is how we came to cross the mountains.

In America it is no uncommon thing for railroads to be built across mountains. But all mountains are not like the Alps, by considerable. Then our American railroads for the most part may be said to go *through* mountains, rather than *over* them; and so are they trying to go through the Alps, or rather under them, in the highest part, by means of a tunnel they are now making, which is to be seven miles long. By means of that tunnel they will be able to avoid the worst part of the route by which we came across. At present the road runs square over high Mont Cenis, which is a rather queer thing for a railroad to do.

You must imagine us then—"Keynote" and myself, for the ladies preferred to stop in Paris—setting out from that city on a certain evening in a kind of lazy snow-storm, which, however, kept us all the while wondering if it snowed on the mountains too. We had arrived at

Paris from London a few days before. Start with us, now, as we get into a "carriage"— that is what they call a "car" in Europe — and wrapping ourselves up in blankets, much as I have seen women roll babies, gradually dropping asleep while the train rushes on. We go south for a while, and then turn a little east. I wonder if you can find Macon on your map of France. That is one of the places where we were. Then we went to a place called Chambery, still farther south and a good deal farther east. There we were among the mountains; in Savoy, where the persecuted Waldenses and Albigenses lived and suffered ages ago. I daresay that they may have had hiding-places among some of these mountains, or may have lived in some of those little valleys that run away up yonder into their depths, as if made on purpose for God's persecuted saints to hide in. But what mountains they were! — not heavily wooded, from base to summit, as many of our American mountains are, but wild, tremendous, awful piles of rocks, heaped up to the very clouds. How stern they looked! And still I loved them, for they have been kind to those to whom man was fierce and cruel, and their rocky hearts are soft and tender compared with the hearts of those who used to chase the poor Christians among them, and throw them down the precipices. Have any of you ever read those lines of Milton, which begin,

"Avenge, O Lord, thy slaughtered saints, whose bones
Lie buried on the Alpine mountains cold."

Among these heights it was, somewhere, that the fierce soldiery of the persecutor would hurl

" Mother with infant down the rocks."

I wonder if the people who live in the villages that nestle here and there, at the base of these great mountains, are like those Waldenses and Albigenses. Their villages are queer-looking things; clusters of very old dwellings, crowded close together, with little bits of windows, and in appearance as if the pigs and chickens were under the same roof with father and mother and Jean and Elizabetta, and quite as much at home. There is a turnip patch, here a little cabbage garden; there the winter wheat is springing up;

and here is a vineyard, the vines stripped of their leaves, but the stakes that held them up still standing. Now and then a group passes along the road near which the railroad runs, plain-looking people, hard-working, evidently, not rich I am very certain — whether they are good I do not know; I hope they are.

But we have yet to cross the mountains, and must not dally and chatter down here, when we are many a long mile from those hardest to get over, and the day, meanwhile — for we have rode all night and another is approaching—wanes fast. Well, here at last we are, at San Michel, and here we must change cars; for such a train as we have come in so far could never get over, nor could such a locomotive as we have had climb the great mountain yonder. So we get into some narrow cars where there is barely room for the people to sit down. This is in order that the train may be as light as possible. If we looked at the track before we got in, we saw perhaps a curious thing; that it had three lines of rails instead of two, the middle one higher than those on the outside. The locomotive, too, if we inspected it, was found to have some additional wheels very curiously placed. They are not fixed edgewise, like other wheels, but are placed with the side down, and are held up above the ground so as not to touch it at all. Their edges are rough, made into teeth, as you might say; and that may help us understand why that third rail which we noticed is all full of notches. If we ask the engineer about it, all he will tell us is, that these horizontal wheels are fixed so as to come on each side of that middle rail, and when he wants them to help pull the train he fixes the machinery so that it makes them clasp the rail, and then turn round like the other wheels, while the teeth play in the notches, and every one as it comes in and out gives a push and so helps the locomotive drag its load along. A man by the name of Fell was determined to have a railroad over these mountains, and that is how he went to work to do it. I am sure that he must be a brave man as well as a skillful one, and I almost think that he ought to spell his name with a T instead of an F. I wonder if you know what makes me think so.

Well, we are not yet over the mountains, nor even started. But at last we get under way.

Up we go. The train stops every few miles, I suppose to get up fresh steam. Up we go. The river, on whose banks we were a little time since, is now far down in the gorge there. The brain almost reels as we look. What a beautiful valley that is, too, down there, with its little village clustering about the plain old church in the midst. Here, near the side of the track, is the entrance to the tunnel they are making, in order to dodge the mountain we shall come to soon; and here, now, is another village, this time clinging to the mountain side, not afraid of the avalanche, though I should think it would be. Up we go, and now we are where for hours back we have seen the thick mist and the snow. In the valley below, it was like an April day, so mild and gentle; here it is winter. Do you see that group of boys? Some of the passengers have thrown out pennies, and they scramble for them just as I have seen a lot of wild chickens when some one has thrown amongst them a handful of corn. There is a little girl holding her apron, as we stop for a while, hoping for a penny; she needs it, poor thing, I dare say. And thus we go on and up, till the snow becomes very deep, and the engine labors and at times nearly stops; but it is plucky, and perseveres; and so at last we reach the mountain top, where the first Emperor Napoleon caused a "hospice" or house of refuge, to be built, in which persons overtaken by storms on the mountain might find shelter. Back a few miles we saw an immensely strong fort, built to guard the pass, and armed, perhaps, even now, with weapons to kill. I believe Napoleon had something to do with that, too. I like this other building much the best; a long, low, but solid one, with plenty of room, and bright lights in some of the windows that glance cheerfully out into the darkness and the storm. Passing this, we soon begin to go down upon the opposite side of the mountain, and in due time are at Susa, which is in Italy, at the southern base of these western Alps. Here we get a supper, and then take a train with the other sort of cars again, and are off for Turin, and Florence, and Rome. And that is how we crossed the mountains.

Now, as I make it out, these several things are necessary in crossing mountains, and I speak of them because crossing mountains is a thing we all have to do some time or other, and it is well to know how.

First. I take it, there must be a way over. Mont Cenis, the mountain which we crossed, is a formidable thing to find in one's path, and I can easily fancy an eagle in some of its rocky heights, screeching defiance in answer to the scream of the locomotive far down below, and scorning the notion that with anything besides wings the great mountain can be passed. But there is a way over it; one that the eagle does not know of. Somewhat like that of which we read, which the vulture's eye hath not seen, and which the lion's whelp hath not trod. It is God who makes the ways over the mountains, and when we have found out where these are we are ready to begin the work of crossing. He would be a fool who should think of running a locomotive, with its train of cars, up the steep, rocky sides of that impassable, huge barrier yonder. Mont Cenis is huge, but it is not impassable, and that makes a vast difference.

Second. Another thing which I suppose to be necessary, in crossing mountains, is the right means for doing it. Down in the valley we can have roomy cars, and long trains, and rush away over the easy track as if railroading was mere boy's play. It is quite another thing when we have mountains to cross. Something of this sort the Apostle Paul seems to have been thinking of when he said, "Let us lay aside every weight, and the sins that do most easily beset us, and let us run with patience the race that is set before us." Any sort of train will do for traveling from one city of worldliness to another, where all the roads are broad and easy, and we can go as swiftly and as smoothly as we like; but if we mean to cross those mountains of difficulty which tower up between us and heaven, we must go about it in quite another way.

Third. Another thing necessary in crossing a mountain is *that we cross it.* This may seem a queer thing to say, but I say it with reason. If you are going over a mountain you must face it, with all its difficulties, take the road *up*, not the road *down*, put on steam and go ahead. The extraordinary way in which some people cross mountains makes me astonished. They will pretend to be going over, when they are just sitting by the roadside whittling sticks.

They will pretend to be crossing, when with their faces toward the base, not the summit, and will call those people silly who imagine that there can be any difficulty in getting over a mountain. Why, they can do it, and not go up hill a single step! Such as these are those people who think, or try to, that they and everybody else will be saved without working out their salvation, by any effort at all. They can not imagine what Paul could be thinking of when he spoke about doing these things "with fear and trembling," it is so easy to be saved. Easy it is to be lost, and so, I fear, multitudes of these deluded ones may some day find.

Fourth. The last thing which I mention is having faith in the conductor. Our conductor was a noisy fellow, but he knew what he was about; so did the engineer, a headstrong Englishman. We had a good deal of faith in them; and when the high walls of snow on either side of the track would almost press against the windows of the car, reaching higher than the car itself, and the engine would puff and falter, and seem just ready to stop, we said, "They'll take us through." And so they did. I am glad that the conductor of our train knew more about crossing mountains than I did, or ever shall. And I am glad that as I try to get over these big mountains between me and heaven, I can confide in one who knows the way I take. Faith in him does, in a certain sense, "remove mountains;" that is, it causes them to be insurmountable obstacles no longer. Mont Cenis stands where it has stood for thousands of years. It frowns as sternly; it thunders and storms as ever before. But men have mastered it, and have compelled it to be a highway and a thoroughfare. Jesus does not annihilate the difficulty that is in the way of man's salvation. He takes us over it; and forever and forever, from the eternal city — much more truly an "Eternal City" than this where I am writing my letter to-night — we shall look back, as I now look back on Mont Cenis, and adore, more and more, the grace that saved us, as we realize what "amazing grace" it was.

UNCLE JOHN.

LETTER FIFTH.

THE TWO CEMETERIES.

Dear Boys and Girls:

 SUPPOSE that the youngest of you know what cemeteries are. Although they are places where the dead are buried, they are yet quite often places which it is very pleasant to visit. It was a happy thought when people began to realize how much may be done to take away the gloom of even death by surrounding the homes of the dead with pleasant scenes, and to consider how much easier they may find it to feel reconciled to the loss of beloved ones, if, visiting them where they lie, they can see the green leaves shining over them, the smooth turf roofing their narrow house, and sweet flowers near.

Such cemeteries, too, are interesting places to visit for other reasons. I want to tell you of two, very widely apart, very unlike in many things, but full of interest, which I have seen; one in London, the other at Rome.

There are two names that you and I have learned to love, one of them especially; two men of whom we hear, perhaps, as often as of any other, save the Bible men. Both had the name of John — John Bunyan and John Wesley. I can remember, also, meeting in my reading with the names of two localities, once in the suburbs of London, now almost in one of its most crowded districts — Moorfields and Bunhill Fields. In the time when John Wesley, his brother Charles, and that wonderful preacher, George Whitefield, were living, Moorfields was quite like a country place. The people dwelling there and thereabouts were poor, ignorant and rude. Whitefield and the Wesleys used to gather them together by hundreds in the open air for preaching, and although they were thought a dangerous people to go amongst, and especially to preach to about their sins, still these good men were not afraid of them, but declared faithfully the truth as it is in Jesus, so that numbers of them were converted.

In process of time a chapel was built there, in which Charles Wesley, the brother of John, and the author of a great many beautiful hymns, preached for a long time, and where John Wesley himself used to preach frequently. The last Sunday which I spent in London I went in the morning to this chapel. I saw the same pulpit which the Wesleys used, and heard a man preach a sermon in it. I saw in the vestry the arm-chair in which John Wesley used to sit, and on the walls of the chapel were tablets, or stones with inscriptions, commemorating the excellences and the services of the two men I have named, with Richard Watson, Jacob Bunting, Robert Newton, and others. At the back of the chapel and on one side is what the English people call a church-yard; that is, it is the enclosure in which the church or the chapel stands, and where they bury the dead. In the portion of the yard that is back of the chapel is a large granite monument, very plain, but very becoming to its purpose, on which is a long inscription. I copied a part of it which reads thus:

> *To the Memory of*
> *The venerable* JOHN WESLEY, A.M.
> *Late Fellow of Lincoln College, Oxford;*
> *This great light arose*
> *(By the singular Providence of God)*
> *To enlighten these realms,*
> *And to revive, enforce and defend*
> *The pure apostolic doctrine and preaching of*
> *The primitive church;*
> *Which he continued to do both by his writings and*
> *his lips*
> *For more than half a century.*
> *And to his inexpressible joy,*
> *Not only beheld their influence extended,*
> *But their efficacy witnessed*
> *In the hearts and lives of many thousands.*

The inscription in the chapel states that Wesley was born June 17, 1703, and died March 2, 1791. He was thus at his death eighty-eight years old. Sixty-five of these he had spent in the ministry of the Gospel, and fifty-two of them as an itinerant preacher. I am not a Methodist, and yet I love John Wesley's name and memory. He was a great man, and what is much better, a good man, and the crown he wears in heaven must be all sparkling with starry gems, for he turned very many indeed to righteousness.

Just across the street from this chapel is what is called Bunhill Fields. It does not seem much like going into the fields to go there, any more than it does at Moorfields. The name, too, seems a singular one, and the way it originated is no less so. It seems that when the present St. Paul's church, in London, was built, being considerably larger than old St. Paul's, which had been burned, (this was in the time of Charles II., and more than two hundred years ago), it had to be extended over what had been the old church-yard. Here a large number of persons had been buried long before, and as no stones had been placed over them nobody knew who they were. In digging for the foundations of new St. Paul's it became necessary to disturb these remains. So they were taken up and carried to the place I tell you of and there buried again. From this circumstance the place was called " Bonehill Fields," which in time became Bunhill Fields.

This, as I told you, is directly across the street from Wesley Chapel. And here, with some others whom I shall name soon, the mother of John and Charles Wesley is buried. The stone now at her grave is a very plain one. It has an inscription, which states that she "was the daughter of Rev. Samuel Annesley, D.D., ejected by the act of uniformity from the Rectory of St. Giles, Cripplegate, August 24, 1662. She was the mother of seventeen children, of whom the most eminent were John and Charles Wesley; the former of whom was, under God, the founder of the people called Methodists.

"'In sure and steadfast hope to rise,
And claim her mansion in the skies,
A Christian here her flesh laid down,
The cross exchanging for a crown.'"

I said that the stone placed over her is small and plain. They are raising money to build a better one, and I had the pleasure of contributing a small sum to this object.

But there is another thing at Bunhill Fields that interested me more than anything else there, or even than what I saw at the other place over the way; this was the tomb of John Bunyan. It is of common gray stone; in form like a large stone chest, with the lid projecting at the edges. Upon the flat top is a figure, or effigy, of Bunyan, lying upon his back, with an open Bible in his left hand. On each side of the monument is a figure of Christian, as represented in the Pilgrim's Progress. In one of them he is just setting out from the City of Destruction, carrying the heavy burden of his sins; in the other he has arrived at the Cross. and as he looks up at it the burden drops from his back and rolls away into an open sepulchre, never to be seen again. At one end of the monument is this simple inscription:

JOHN BUNYAN,
Author of "Pilgrim's Progress,"
Died 1688, aged 60.

That is all, and it is quite enough. At the other end one reads that this monument was "restored by public subscription under the presidency of the Right Honorable the Earl of Shaftesbury, May, 1862." This means that the stone had become defaced, and the inscription scarcely legible, on account of its age, and that the figures and words were cut over again, so that they could be plainly seen.

There was also another name at Bunhill Fields which the boys and girls do not know so well as they do that of Bunyan, although a book written by the man who once bore it is almost as popular with them — with some of them I am afraid more popular — than even "Pilgrim's Progress." We had to look for the stone on which this name is chiseled for a good while, it is so small and low, but at last we found it. This is what we read:

DANIEL DEFOE,
*(Author of
Robinson Crusoe),
Who died April* 24, 1781,
In his 70th year.

I do not think that Daniel Defoe was as great a man as John Bunyan, or as good a man, but I was glad to see where his ashes lie, although sorry that a better stone does not mark the spot.

Bunhill Fields, I am compelled to say, is not a pleasant spot. I spoke at the beginning of cemeteries as *now* being made very delightful.

This of which I am speaking is not one of those. I doubt if there is a tree anywhere within the enclosure. I saw no green grass, nor a flower, nor anything to remind of life. Everything spoke only of death, and in its most naked and most forbidding form. All the stones were of the rough gray kind, much blackened by the smoke and the rains, while numbers of the inscriptions were so worn that it was impossible to read them. Quite different, in these respects, is the cemetery which I have visited to-day, and which is the other one of the two I proposed to write you about. It is here at Rome, fifteen hundred miles away from London; here, in Catholic Rome, but a *Protestant* cemetery.

Shall I tell you when I determined that if I came to Rome I would visit this cemetery? It was some months ago, after reading in a certain book that, according to the most reliable accounts, it was here that the apostle Paul was beheaded. Perhaps you know that some distance away from Rome, and at the mouth of the Tiber, is Ostia, which used to be quite an important place, though now very far from being so. It was the *port* of Rome, where all the vessels came, where the grain was brought from foreign countries to supply the great city, and where the ships of war, with their soldiers and sailors on board, would sail in and out. There was a road, one of the noble Roman roads, made from the city to Ostia, a distance of fifteen miles. The road passes through one of the city gates, in the wall now so old and moss-covered, and runs near the river on to where the old port used to be. Once it was thronged as it now never is with marching soldiers, with sailors on leave from their ships, with teams bringing grain, with groups of horsemen, perhaps a Roman knight and his escort; with a busy multitude, and at all hours of the day.

The road I have described runs along the river for quite a distance before it passes through the gate and so begins to leave the city. For much of the way, too, it is through open tracts, or where the houses are very sparse and the trees are growing. Near the gate in the wall there is a tall pyramid, built of square stone. The wall runs up to it on each side, and is built against it, so that the pyramid seems to make part of the wall, although much higher. It was erected about the commencement of the Christian era, and so is almost nineteen hundred years old. It was built as the monument of Caius Cestius, a Roman, and one of the magistrates of the city. Now the book I was reading, "Conybeare and Howson's Life of St. Paul," says that the most probable account of the death of the great apostle is, that he was led out towards the outer wall of the city along the Ostian road, and near the base of that pyramid was beheaded. At the same time that I went to the place I am describing, I passed still farther on till almost a mile beyond the city wall, and there I saw and entered a magnificent church, under the altar of which they say that both Paul and Timothy are buried. I am sure I do not know whether they are so or not. But it was thrilling to be there and think even that they *might* be.

Now it is close by that pyramid of Cestius, on the side of the wall towards the city, and close up to it, that the Protestant cemetery is. It is not large, neither is it laid out so handsomely as a great many in our American cities; but it is a quiet, pleasant spot, and men are employed to keep the walks neat, the hedges nicely trimmed, and to see that no one defaces or injures any thing there. The persons buried there are mostly those who came to Rome, as I have, to visit it, or perhaps to live for a few years, and were taken sick and died. They were, I noticed, from America, from England, Ireland, Scotland, Holland, Germany, and other countries. Among them is the wife of Hon. Lewis Cass, who used to live in Michigan, in his life an eminent statesman. She was a daughter of Hon. John A. King, another eminent American. On one monument I read, "He giveth his beloved sleep;" on another, "Weeping may endure for a night, but joy cometh in the morning;" on another, that of a young girl of fourteen, "Because I live ye shall live also." Very unlike these is that upon the stone that marks the grave of John Keats, who wrote, while he lived, such beautiful poetry, but died so unhappily:

"This grave contains all that was mortal of a young English poet, who, on his death-bed, in the bitterness of his heart at the malicious power of his enemies, desired these words to be written upon his tombstone: 'Here lies one whose name was writ in water.' Feb. 24, 1821."

How much better it is to be a Christian, and "sleep" as one of the Lord's "beloved," than to be the best poet that ever lived, without this! Shelley, another English poet, is also buried here.

It would be nice to know whether this is really the place where Paul was beheaded. I almost feel sure that it was. Returning to the city I passed over ground where perhaps his own feet trod. He may have looked back upon the towers and dwellings of the city, and seen them much as I saw them, perhaps with a sorrow like that of Jesus as he wept over Jerusalem. I know that he went bravely, not afraid to die; for had he not written, perhaps only a day or two before, "I am now ready to be offered, and the time of my departure is at hand. I have fought a good fight, I have finished my course, I have kept the faith; henceforth there is laid up for me a crown of righteousness, which the Lord, the righteous Judge, shall give me; and not to me only, but to all them who love his appearing." Paul, Bunyan, the Wesleys, and many a one besides, are wearing that crown. Is there one preparing for each of us, dear young friends? God grant that it may be so, is the prayer of

UNCLE JOHN.

LETTER SIXTH.

CHRISTMAS IN PARIS.

DEAR BOYS AND GIRLS:

PERHAPS I had better not tell you the name of the person who wrote the jingle which I shall ask the editor at home to print in this letter. But as he uses several French words, I must tell you what they mean. *Garçon* (pronounce the *ç* like an *s*) is "waiter;" *fille* is "maid-servant;" *Madame* is the title usually given to the lady in charge of a French lodging-house; *recherché* is "stylish;" *bon jour* is "Good-day," or "Good-morning;" *Eh bien* is "well;" *Monsieur*, of course, is "Sir," and is often used in addressing a gentleman, instead of his name; *à Chicago* is "at Chicago;" *à Paris* (pronounced *Paree*,) at Paris.

You know, I suppose, that *carte de visite* is a gentleman's or lady's "card," such as they use in making calls. You may now read what this "poet"—a very poor one I think—tells about his Christmas in Paris, and then I will tell you about mine.

On the morning of Christmas, as musing I sat
In my lodgings at Paris, upon the third flat,
And wondering if Christmas would be as of yore,
As bright and as glad — came a knock at the door.
Assured 'twas the *garçon*, the *fille*, or *Madame*,
I opened, and there stood a spruce little man.
From his toe to his top he was perfect in style;
Not a stain on his boot, not a scratch on his tile;
Not a wrinkle to mar the superlative set
Of waistcoat or coat, or *recherché* cravat.
One hand wore its glove, the other was bare,
That the public might notice the diamond rings there.
This flourished a cane, *that* was held ready
To do the polite to a gent or a lady.
One fault in his *physique* I could not but see;
A fop should be slender, but not so was he.
In fact, though the word would perhaps have appalled him,
His rigging apart, I should surely have called him
Some rubicund Dutchman abroad for his beer,
Or Old Christmas, himself, thus early astir.

Quite crushed by such elegance, while I stood mute,
"*Bon jour*," said my friend with a killing salute;

"*Monsieur*, I crave pardon, so early a guest,
But allow me to wish ' Merry Christmas,' at least."
Recalled to my senses, I hastened to say,
" Walk in, sir, walk in, and be seated I pray;
On the sofa, I beg, and kindly, dear sir,
Receive my best thanks for the grace you confer."
Quite briskly and gaily he entered, and took
The seat I had offered, then airily spoke,
While under the smirk on his shining, fat face,
A something familiar I now seemed to trace :
" Monsieur does not know me, I plainly can see;
My *carte de visite*, if I make not too free."
On the finest card-paper, and daintily set
In gilt edges and flourishes bright and complete,
Bewildered and wondering, half out of my head—
You will scarcely believe it. 'twas this that I read :
" *Santa Claus, chez lui, à la Rue Rivoli
Numero cinquante-neuf; venez a dinde rotie.*"*
" You see, Monsieur, we're not strangers at all,
Nor is this the first time I have made you a call.
It should not make us strangers, that this side the sea
We meet, not *à Chicago*, but instead *à Paris*.'
" Dear friend, pray excuse me," I stammering began,
" But in truth, I—I—." "Yes," said the gay little man,
" I know what you mean; you think strange
Of this which to you seems a marvelous change.
You ask, 'Where are the reindeers, the sleigh, and the driver?'
And it seems like the arts of some conjuring contriver,
Santa Claus turned a Frenchman in broadcloth and rings,

    * " Santa Claus, at home, at the street Rivoli,
      Number fifty-nine; come to roast turkey."

And fine in himself, not dispensing fine things."
"It is true—I confess—." I was stammering once more,
When "Pardon, Monsieur," he burst in as before,
"No apology needed, and indeed on my side
Explanation is due, and must not be denied.
For all that you've known of your friend, Santa Claus,
One thing you'll now learn, and in this find the cause
Of what has surprised you; my journeys so wide,
Round the world, make it needful that I should provide
Against much misconstruction, by becoming, you see,
All things to all men, so far as may be.
So in France I'm a Frenchman, in Germany Dutch,
In England John Bullish, though not overmuch.
In Spain I'm a Spaniard, in Mexico too;
And in short, when in Rome do as all Romans do."
"I see, yes, I see," I replied much relieved;
"And still, in America, much as you've lived,
You will pardon my saying it seems rather strange
That when you are with us, we see no such change."
"And perhaps you will tell me," he said in reply,
"Since the whole world is there even more than am I,
What nation you are, and what one must become,
To make himself like you, and be quite at home.
Is it Irish, Norwegian, or Chinese, or what?
For indeed it's a puzzle to tell what you're not.
So I think it must answer, since all will do so,
To be just myself, as I come and I go."
"And what could be better, dear friend?" I replied;
"Be Santa Claus still, our delight and our pride.
For myself, scarcely aught gives me homesickness more,
Than to think I'll not hear, as of old, at my door,

Or above on the roof the light hoofs of the team,
Or along the white drifts see it glide like a dream."
"*Eh bien, Monsieur,*" here he broke in again,
"We'll dismiss, please, this quite un-Parisian strain,
And I must be off, but before I shall go,
As of old I've been wont in my visits to do,
Let me leave you my gift, it is exquisite stuff,
Please take, Monsieur, *a pinch of my snuff.*"

With a twirl of his moustache, a whisk of his cane,
He walked to the door, and whistling a strain
Of the latest grand opera, went on his way;
And left me to muse and discuss all the day,
"Will the host, or his cookery, puzzle me most?
Shall I go to his dinner, and taste of his roast?"

The question seems to have remained unanswered, since here the "poem" ends; and so, much to my regret, I can tell you nothing as to how they cook and eat roast turkey at Santa Claus' French lodging-house. Your Christmas, dear young friends, will have been past some days when you read this, and still you will not have forgotten how *your* roast turkey tasted. For myself, I had none; neither did anybody here in the house where I am living just now wish any other body a "Merry Christmas." It is not the custom in Paris, although they do have the "Happy New Year." They give

Christmas presents, too, sometimes, but generally I think reserve those for New Year's; at which time, possibly, Santa Claus may be more like himself, and give his friends, when he comes to see them, something better than a pinch of snuff!

Some things about Christmas, here in Paris, I must tell you. It was a good deal more, in one respect, like Sunday, than Sunday itself ever is; that is to say, the stores and other places of business were closed, as very few of them are upon the Sabbath. The French people — and indeed the people generally upon the continent of Europe, that is in other portions besides Great Britain — know very little about the Sabbath, except as a day to go to church in, if they like, and to rest from labor and enjoy pleasure excursions, if they choose so to do. An American, English, or Scottish Sabbath one never finds south of the English channel. But certain other days in the year are honored as the Sabbath is not. Of these there are four, Christmas, All-Saints' Day, Easter and Whitsuntide. At some of the churches in Paris, mass, the most important and solemn of all the Catholic services, was being celebrated all Christmas day, from early in the morning till late at evening. It was so at the Madeleine, and as we were there at the eleven o'clock mass, I must tell you a few things about what I saw and heard.

The Madeleine is a very large and very beautiful church, dedicated to Mary Magdalene, called by the Catholics *Saint* Mary Magdalene; Madeleine being the French word for Magdalene. The church contains various pictures and statues which I have not time now to describe. I must tell you, however, about the beautiful marble group, which one sees just behind where the priests officiate — what is called "the altar." It represents Mary Magdalene borne to heaven by angels, while at the corners in front other angels are kneeling, as if in adoration. The figures are very beautiful, but I am sure that the Mary Magdalene spoken of in the New Testament would have felt very sorry if she had known that some time or other she would be represented in such a way, and made to bear a part in what seems so much like idolatry.

The service was very lengthy, and with the exception of the fine music, to us very tedious;

for it was mostly without meaning. Whenever any of the officiating priests prayed, they turned their backs to the people, and spoke only in whispers, or at least so as not to be heard. When they read from the Scripture they *chanted*, or sang it, in the Latin language, so that very few persons, if any, understood. But the prayers and the reading, such as they were, made but a small part of the ceremony, which consisted mostly in marching about in procession, sometimes carrying candles, sometimes the prayer-books, in kneeling down and rising up, in swinging the censers with the incense smoking, and such like things, which to us had not the least particle of *worship* in them. Twenty-five different persons officiated, perhaps ten or twelve of them priests, in robes covered with rich gold embroidery. The rest were boys, some of whom were dressed in red capes and hoods over white robes; while four had on only the white robes, with blue sashes round the waist, hanging down at the side. These were the incense-bearers. Sometimes they would all be before the altar, arranging themselves, now in a square, now in a different kind of figure, and then marching off to the right and left. At other times only portions of them would be present.

A Catholic mass is what I never tried to understand, and this one was, therefore, wholly senseless to me, whatever it may have been to others. The singing, only, and the instrumental music we enjoyed. The choir, a very large one, and made up wholly of men and boys, was behind the altar — which towered up very high — and so was mostly out of sight. These singers were accompanied by a full orchestra, or band, of stringed instruments, including a harp. At the other end of the church was an organ, and in some parts of the service it would respond, very finely, to the choir and instruments by the altar. At one part they sang "the Portuguese Hymn," which in our country has the words, "The Lord is our Shepherd." It was the only thing, from first to last, which we could understand, or which we in the least enjoyed. We came down the broad, noble steps of the Madeleine, even more thoroughly Protestant than when we went up.

Another service held in Paris on this Christmas day was quite a contrast with the one I have described. The place was very different; — not a magnificent church facing down a wide street, with noble columns in front and on either side, and adorned within with frescoes, gilding, painting and statuary, but a small chapel, in the third story of a building on one side of a secluded court, entered from a narrow street. The street has a name quite appropriate, I think, considering who they are that meet in this chapel. It is the Rue des Bons Enfants — Street of the Good Children; and those who meet at the place I now tell you of are, I hope, many of them, true children of God. They are the French Baptist church, congregation and Sunday-school. The church numbers about eighty, but a good many besides the members attend, so that often their chapel is crowded. Last Sabbath, when I was there, all the seats were filled. To be sure, the place is not large, holding not over a hundred and fifty; yet to me it was far more "the house of God," and far nearer to "the gate of heaven," than was the magnificent Madeleine, or than the still more magnificent St. Peter's, in Rome, seemed when I was in it so often a few days ago.

On the afternoon of Christmas three were baptized at the French chapel. They had a sermon, then the baptism, after that the communion. It was a good way to celebrate Christmas, was it not? They have no baptisteries in this chapel, and so were obliged to use a large bath-tub. Some one asked why they did not go to the river, the Seine, which runs through Paris, and would be readily reached from the chapel. The answer was that they would not be allowed to do so. A generous gentleman, Mr. Carpenter, of Boston, who has been spending some time in Paris, suggested to them, on the occasion of a former baptism, that they should go to the river, and offered to meet the expense of carriages for that purpose. He was told that while the Government permit the Baptist, and other Protestant congregations, to hold meetings, if they do it quietly, they will not suffer them to do any thing that would attract public attention like a baptism in the river. This reminds me to tell you that the Baptists in Paris and in other parts of France have formerly suffered much annoyance and hindrance from the jealousy of the Government, which is Catholic so far as it is anything. At present, however, they are "tolerated" if they will not be too active and prominent. Even this is something; although I think that the very idea of "tolerating" men in worshiping God according to their consciences, is an insult to human rights. It is very much like "tolerating" men in eating their dinners. Truly, it is a great thing to *permit* us (which is what toleration means) to do what we have a perfect right to do, anyhow!

On Wednesday evening following Christmas they had a Christmas tree for the Sunday-school children at the French chapel. The school is not large, but those connected with branch schools in the city were present, and these, with the grown people, filled the chapel quite full. The tree was very brilliant, covered with little tapers and with gay presents, dolls and other toys, while the more valuable ones, books and such like, were kept out of sight elsewhere till the time came to distribute them. When I went in, Rev. Mr. Lepoids, one of the pastors of the church, was making an address. He was followed by Rev. Mr. Van Meter, from New York, and he by Mr. Dez, the other pastor. These addresses were interspersed with singing. They sang, too, while the presents were being handed round. One of the tunes was our "Happy Land," and it was like home to hear them singing it. They very kindly remembered Uncle John and Aunt Esther, giving each a "*Souvenir de Noel*," — that is, Souvenir of Christmas, "Noel" being the word which the French use for the holiday that is so much a favorite everywhere.

UNCLE JOHN.

PLACE DE LA CONCORDE.

LETTER SEVENTH.

THE STORY OF A KING.

DEAR BOYS AND GIRLS:

I FREQUENTLY pass, as I go to and fro, in this city of Paris, a tall, slender shaft of stone, like a monument, running nearly to a point at the top, and, long as it is, made of a single block, with the exception of the pedestal upon which it stands. It is covered, from base to top, with very singular looking characters, called "hieroglyphics." This is what they term an "obelisk." It was found some years ago among the ruins of an ancient Egyptian city, called Thebes, and was brought from there about thirty years since, and placed where it now is, by Louis Philippe, then the king of France. As one stands by this obelisk, looking toward the river Seine, not far away, upon his right hand a noble avenue stretches off, with rows of trees, and other wide avenues, parallel with it, on either side, up to a large structure, in the form of an immense arch, which they call the "Arc de Triomphe," erected by Napoleon I. Upon the left, down another avenue, one sees the palace of the Tuileries. This other avenue runs through the Garden of the Tuileries, which is very large and spacious, and covered with trees, statuary and fountains.

Upon the spot where the obelisk I have described stands, a very sad and wicked thing was done on the morning of Jan. 21, 1793. A vast crowd was gathered here on that morning, surrounding this spot and stretching far away, covering especially all the elevated places from which a view of what was going forward could be had. Nearest to the central point I have mentioned, only the soldiers were seen. Their orders were to keep back the crowd, and prevent them from pressing upon the vacant space within. Vacant, but not wholly so; for in the centre of it was a scaffold, or platform, covered with black cloth, upon one part of which was a strange looking thing, whose name was destined ere long to become ominous and fearful to a whole nation — the Guillotine. Two upright pieces were joined above and below, making a perpendicular frame, while in grooves prepared in those upright parts a sharp, heavy knife was made to run, so that when raised to the top and then suddenly released, it would fall like lightning, with its edge upon a block placed below. Thousands upon thousands of the population of Paris had assembled, on this morning, to witness what some trembled even to think of, what others expected with a fierce joy.

And thousands more were in the streets by which this spot — then called the Place de la Revolution, now the Place de la Concorde — was approached from the side opposite to the river. In this direction a carriage was slowly drawing near. It had set out some two hours before from a gloomy, castle-like building, called the Temple, a long way off, and so crowded were the streets through which it passed, that it had been compelled to move as a hearse moves to a burial. These crowds were all armed men. The Government had ordered that every person found anywhere along that route unarmed should be at once arrested. All who could have felt any sympathy for the person whom the carriage I have mentioned contained, or any commiseration for his fate, were thus shut up in their homes, while only his ferocious and implacable enemies were to be seen, as now on this side, now on that, he would raise his eyes to look out at the window.

Three persons were in the carriage besides himself. Two of these were guards; the other was a priest. The priest, the Abbé Edgeworth de Firmont, had handed him a prayer-book, from which he read portions of Scripture, especially the Psalms, and some of the prayers. The drums were beating, the crowd hooting and roaring, the cavalry keeping guard before and behind tramping noisily — altogether it was like the tumult of a tempest, and as it was impossible to converse, the time of the long, slow, dreadful ride was passed in reading those inspired words, and in lifting up to heaven requests for comfort and for salvation which we cannot but hope were not without some true faith in Jesus, nor unheard. The person of whom I thus speak was a man thirty-nine years of age, with a mild, kind face, and a dignity in his manner that proved he was no common man, and might easily make one doubt if he could possibly be a criminal, or deserving of such a death as they had prepared for him. At last the carriage stopped.

"We are there, unless I deceive myself," said this person to the priest, who accompanied him. The priest could not answer, so overcome was he by his emotion. Three men came forward and opened the door of the carriage, and the two guards, rising, were about to step out, when the person whom they had thus brought stopped them, and laying his hand upon the knee of the priest who sat by his side, said, in the tone of one accustomed to command:

"I recommend to you this gentleman. Take care that after my death no injury or insult be offered to him. I charge you to have a care for this."

One of the three men who had come to open the door smiled in a grim way and said: "Be easy, we shall take care of him, never fear."

The occupants of the carriage then descended. The person of whom I have spoken, repulsing the offer of the three men to aid him, removed his coat, and took off his collar, so as to leave his neck bare. The men were then about to bind him, when he drew back proudly, and exclaimed,

"What are you about to do?"

"To bind you," said one of them.

"To bind me?" he replied. "I will never consent to that. Do with me what you have been commanded to do; but you shall never bind me."

The three men prepared to lay hands on him and bind him by main force, and he was preparing to resist them, when looking toward the priest, that good man said to him, as well as he could, in the midst of his weeping:

"Sire, in this new outrage I see only a last trait of resemblance between your majesty and the God of Calvary, who is soon to be your recompense."

"Ah," said he, "nothing less than this example could induce me to submit to such an affront. Do what you will; I will drink the cup to its dregs."

They bound his hands, and he then ascended the steps of the scaffold, leaning upon the arm of the priest. Having reached the top, he walked by himself to the centre of the platform, and casting one look along the beautiful avenue to the palace where he had lived so long, he signed with his hand for the drums, which were beating, to stop, and then, advancing to the front of the platform, said:

"Frenchmen, you see your king here, upon the scaffold. I pardon the authors of my death, and I desire that the blood you are about to shed may profit you, and may never fall back upon France!"

Here the man, named Sartine, who was directing this hideous business, exclaimed to the executioner:

"Do your work, and you, drummers, to your drums!" The voice of the king was drowned. He attempted no more words, but walking to the instrument of death placed his head upon the block, while, as the axe descended, the priest exclaimed, "Son of St. Louis, ascend to heaven!"

I have almost doubted, since I began this recital, if I ought to tell you a story that is so very sad and harrowing; but it is a part of this world's sorrowful history, and sooner or later you must learn not only of this, but of a great many other things equally dreadful. The king I have been telling you of was Louis Sixteenth, the king of France. He had been a king nineteen years. There are many who say that if he had had more firmness and resolution he might have saved his own crown and life, and protected his kingdom from the horrors that followed, in the Reign of Terror. I doubt it; but, if he had not all the strength needful for such a charge in such a time, he was at least a good man, and that was more than could have been said of any king of France for many a long century. Indeed, I think, that, as so often happens, and as *must* happen unless God prevents it by miracles, he suffered for the crimes and follies of those who had reigned before him. The patience of the nation had been worn out with the wrongs done them by former kings, and they did not realize that *they* were the guilty ones, not he. Besides, it was a time when very bad men had gained the power in France. They were ambitious to have things all their own way. The king was an obstacle, and it was thus they removed him!

For my part, I love to think of Louis Sixteenth, and of his wife, Marie Antoinette, who suffered a like death only a few months later, and nearly upon the same spot, as they were in their youth, and in the first days of their marriage. His father, Louis Fifteenth, and her mother, Marie Theresa, Empress of Austria, were then both living. At the time of their marriage he was sixteen years of age, and she fifteen — a young couple, but a happy one. They lived in the beautiful palace of Versailles, about fifteen miles out of Paris, and, while experiencing what many esteem the highest and happiest human condition, showed by various acts, one of which I will relate to you, that they could think of other things besides their own pleasure.

On the 30th of June, 1770, the city of Paris gave a grand entertainment in honor of young Louis, the Dauphin (as the eldest son of the king was always called), and his wife, whose marriage had then recently taken place. By a sad casualty, which occurred in the midst of the rejoicings, several persons were killed. Learning of this next day, Louis wrote this letter to the Prefect of Police:

"Monsieur Sartine, I am filled with sorrow at the calamities of which I learn. They tell me that through your failure to make sure that public security with which you were charged, several persons have fallen victims to a casualty near the close of the *fete* which the good city of Paris has believed itself bound to give on the occasion of my marriage. Ah! my grief is more profound than I can express to you at this moment. I am about to receive my annuity, and I send it to you at once, for the assistance of those who suffer, and of the unhappy relatives of those who have been killed. L. DAUPHIN."

There were other similar acts which showed his kind heart, and when, in 1774, upon the death of his father, he ascended the throne, the French people felt sure that they had a good king. How he and his young queen felt, you may infer from the fact that on learning of his father's death, he and Marie Antoinette fell upon their knees, while he cried out, "My God, protect us. We are too young to reign. I am a king while yet only twenty years of age. What a burden! What a calamity!" I am sure that it was at least his wish and his endeavor, from that time till he died, as I told you, on the scaffold in the Place de la Revolution, to be a good king.

LETTER EIGHTH.

THE STORY OF A KING.—CONCLUDED.

DEAR BOYS AND GIRLS:

 MUST now tell you of some things that took place after that January morning, in 1793. All the friends of the king, not only, but the ministers of religion as well, felt themselves in danger after such an event; the latter, because the anger of the people had been excited as much against the priesthood as against the monarchy. I am sorry to say that the priests were not such men as the ministers of religion ought to be, and that much of what they taught for religion was false, and calculated to mislead men, to the ruin of their souls. Some of them, however, were, I think, at least sincere. Most of the priests, with as many of the king's friends as possibly could, escaped

from the country. Others hid themselves in out-of-the-way places in the city, and lived as they might.

A priest, such as I have described, had taken refuge in a very poor, dilapidated dwelling in what is called the Faubourg Saint Martin, one of the oldest parts of Paris. In this mean and comfortless place lived two old women in great poverty, and with them the priest had found shelter. One of these women, on the evening of the same day that King Louis suffered, returning to the house said to her companion, as she hastily entered,

"Hide yourself! hide yourself! Though we go out so seldom, we have still been watched."

"What has happened?" inquired the other.

The woman who had just come in told her that she had been followed by a man who had the appearance of a spy, and that he now stood without watching their dwelling. The old priest, who sat near and heard the conversation, tried to encourage them, but finally consented that they should conceal him as well as they could, as he, not they, was most in danger. They had hardly so done, when they heard the steps of the unknown man upon the stairs. He stopped at the door, and rapped. They were too frightened to make any reply, and after waiting a little time he opened the door and entered. He was a middle-sized man, with an air of melancholy, but nothing in his manner that seemed threatening. He stood for a few moments looking around the room, and at last fixed his eyes upon the two old women who sat trembling with fear. At length he said, in a mild, and even timid tone:

"I do not come here as an enemy. If I disturb or alarm you, speak freely, and I will retire. But know that I am friendly to you, and if there is any service I can render, let me know of it without the least fear."

One of the women, named Agatha, motioned him to take a seat. He did so, and then said:

"I am aware that you have given asylum to a venerable priest, who has miraculously escaped the recent massacres."

The other woman, named Martha, replied hastily, "But, sir, we have no priest here—"

"You should then take better care of what you leave around," said the stranger smiling, as he advanced to the table and took up a priest's breviary.* "I do not think you understand Latin. But fear nothing; for five days I have known of your necessities, and of your devotion to the venerable man to whom you have given a refuge. I only wish to serve both you and him."

At these words the priest himself came from his place of concealment.

"I can not believe, sir," he said, "that you are one of our persecutors. What do you wish of me?"

"I come to ask," replied the stranger, "that you will perform a private mass for the repose of the soul of one — of — a person whose body will not, there is reason to fear, rest in consecrated ground."

It was one of the superstitions of the time that if a person was not buried in ground consecrated by the priests their souls would suffer; also that masses, or prayers, offered for them might do them good. This was what this man

* The "breviary" is the Catholic prayer-book. This was one for the use of priests, and was in the Latin language.

wanted. He did not say who it was for whom he desired the priest to pray, but his allusions left no doubt that it was the king, slaughtered, as I have said, of whom he spoke. After some conversation the priest consented to do as requested, and the stranger left, promising to return again in two hours. At the end of that time he entered the room again in the same manner as before. In the meantime the two aged women had made the necessary preparations; the priest had put on the habiliments customary in such a service, and the four persons united in the ceremony, solemn and impressive at such a moment, however mistaken. While prayer was being offered for the soul of the departed one, the stranger showed great emotion, and when the service was concluded the priest approached him and said:

"My son, if you have dipped your hands in the blood of the martyr-king, place confidence in my words. It is not a fault incapable of pardon where repentance is so sincere as this which you seem to manifest."

"My father," said the man, much affected,

"no one is more innocent than I of the blood shed in the day past."

"I believe you," replied the priest. Further effort to ascertain the reasons of this singular conduct of the man was unavailing. After a little time more he left, first arranging that, in a year from that evening, he would come again, and desiring that a like service might be then performed. At the end of the year he reappeared in the same mysterious manner as before, and at the same hour of midnight. They had everything in readiness, and the mass for the repose of the martyr-king's soul was again celebrated. During the interval, in ways which they were not permitted to understand, the wants of the two old women and their aged guest had been bountifully met. Food, clothing, and other necessary things were found every day placed at their door, and although for a part of the year famine reigned in the city, they themselves never lacked.

The same religious service continued to be celebrated year after year, at the same place, until Napoleon took possession of the government, and necessity for such concealment no longer existed. At each occasion the stranger reappeared, and in the meantime the wants of the priest and the women were supplied. When public worship was re-established, and social order restored, so that the priest could seek out his friends and find other means of support, the mysterious visitor was seen no more.

But the same mass, upon the same day of the year, continued to be observed, although transferred to a church in the vicinity. The bodies of Louis and Marie Antoinette had been removed from the precincts of the Temple, where they were first buried, and placed in a small cemetery near what is now the church of the Madeleine. This was done by command of the wicked men who had caused them to be put to death; and in order that nothing might be left of their remains, they directed that they should be buried in quick-lime, which, it was expected, would consume them. This was done; but the purpose was in a measure disappointed. In 1815, a brother of Louis Sixteenth became king, as Louis Eighteenth. By his command, search was made where the bodies of the king and queen had been placed, and enough was found to identify them. A chapel was erected upon the spot, and while so much of the bodies as had been found were taken to St. Denis, where the kings of France are buried, other things discovered in the same place were put in a stone coffin, or large chest, which now stands in an open crypt, or chamber, beneath the altar of the chapel.

We have visited this chapel, "La Chapelle Expiatoire," as it is called. In the court, or yard, through which we first passed, as we entered, were the graves of the Swiss Guards of Louis Sixteenth, who were killed in his defense at the time when his palace was invaded by the mob. The chapel itself is a small, singular building, but a most interesting place to visit. On one side of the room where service is held is a marble group, representing King Louis upon his knees, sustained by an angel, who points upward to heaven. Upon the other side is another group, representing the Queen, also kneeling, with her eyes fixed upon a cross, which Religion, under the form of Madame Elizabeth, the King's sister, holds out to her. Every thing about the chapel is simple and touching. I felt more impressed than in any other place which I have seen in Europe. I said to the guide, as we stood looking at the stone coffin, of which I spoke, "*Louis Seize était un bon homme*," (Louis Sixteenth was a good man.)

"*Oui, Monsieur*," (Yes, sir,) he replied.

"*Et aussi un bon Roi*," (And a good King, too.)

"*Oui, Monsieur*," (Yes, sir), he said again, while his eyes filled with tears.

But who was the mysterious stranger? Long years after it was ascertained that he was one of those who had been compelled by an office which he held to assist at the execution of Louis Sixteenth. He had done so against his will, and only because a refusal would have cost him his life. He had been touched with a pity and sorrow, which he manifested in the way I have described. I need not tell you that this idea of praying for the souls of the dead is a mere superstition; nor that the hope of this man to expiate by such means the act, however compulsory, which he remembered with such pain, was altogether a mistaken one. You all know well that what is done for the soul's happiness *hereafter* must be done *here*, and by the soul itself; also that the pardon of sin comes only through prayer in the name of Jesus. I have, however, told you this story of a King that you may have something to remind you what reasons to be thankful American boys and girls have that they live in a country where such things as I have described are not done; and also to be thankful that in the lessons of Christian homes and of the Sabbath-school, they are taught a true religion, and not the fables and superstitions that only deceive.

Uncle John.

LETTER NINTH.

THE BIRDS IN THE PALACE GARDEN.

Dear Boys and Girls:

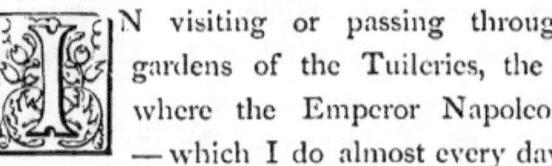N visiting or passing through the gardens of the Tuileries, the palace where the Emperor Napoleon lives — which I do almost every day when I am well — I have often witnessed a very beautiful thing. I must tell you that this garden is in two parts. One is for the use of those who live in the palace, exclusively; no one else ever ventures there. This is much smaller than the other part, although still very large. It is beautifully laid out in walks, with fountains in different parts, and has a great deal of shrubbery. It is separated from the larger portion by a handsome iron fence, ex-

cept at the centre, where there is a large iron gate and a wide carriage-drive, by which the Emperor and Empress, often, as they return from their ride in the streets of Paris, in their carriage with four horses and out-riders, enter. At this gate there are always at least two soldiers on guard.

The other part of the garden is much larger. It is almost like a park, containing acres of ground, planted with trees, with little grass-plats and flower-beds in different parts, while at each end is a magnificent fountain whose water, as it falls, makes a large pond, on which the boys skate and slide in winter, and sail their little boats in summer. For into this part of the gardens any one who pleases may come and stay as long as he likes; may stroll about and look at the statues, of which there are a great number, or sit under the trees, or play at ball or other games — in short, it is a real pleasure-ground. On a pleasant day you would be always sure to find a great number of persons there, in bright dresses, many of them, some walking, some sitting, some engaged in games of different sorts; nurses, with little babies in their arms, little boys and girls, in regular troops, soldiers, citizens, and now and then a sick man, like Uncle John, walking slowly along with the help of his cane. The women, except the well-dressed ladies, almost all wear a funny little white cap, always as clean as it can be, and very pretty, especially when there is a smiling happy face under it.

Now, on the Emperor's side of the iron fence, I spoke of, and near the wall, there is, as I said, a great deal of shrubbery, kept in the nicest order by the men in charge of the garden, and in those trees a great number of birds have their home. They are wonderfully tame, and do not seem in the least afraid of the people who are always thronging about. The pretty sight I spoke of, is to see these little birds fly up, as they will, and take their food from the hands of persons who seem often to come there almost on purpose to feed them. I have seen a man stand, and making a little chirping noise, call the birds to him, and while he held out to them a crumb of bread between his thumb and finger, the little creatures would fly to him, catch it and rush away, as if astonished at their own audacity. Sometimes, as they fluttered and circled about him, he would throw the crumbs up into the air, and the swift little birds would dart upon and snatch them before they fell to the ground. Often, too, I have seen the children feeding them as they might a group of chickens. I have stopped, many and many a time, to see what I have described, for it was pretty to look at, and made me think of some things that I love to remember.

I did not find out the name of these little birds in the palace gardens for some time; but one day I asked the landlady of the hotel where we live, what they are called. "*Moineaux*," said she, for she speaks no English — "Sparrows."

I was glad when I heard they were sparrows; for it was about the sparrows that I had been thinking. I remembered first, indeed, that passage, which says, "Behold the fowls of the air," that is, the birds, "they sow not, neither do they reap, nor gather into barns; *yet your Heavenly Father feedeth them. Are ye not much better than they?*" Will not God feed you, and take care of you, who are of so much more consequence in his sight? But I had thought, also, of those other verses: "Are not five sparrows sold for two farthings? And one of them shall not fall on the ground without your Father"—without your Father taking notice of it. "But even the very hairs of your head are numbered." I had thought, too, of that place in the Psalms, where David says, one time when he is feeling very badly, "I am like a sparrow alone upon the house-top." The sparrows are wonderfully social little birds. They seem to love each other's society very much, keep in groups, or if they fly off somewhere, rarely fly alone. I imagined one of them, for some reason, living alone upon the top of the high palace yonder, perhaps driven away by his mates; perhaps seeking solitude, because unhappy; or perhaps too proud to associate with common birds. How unlike the merry little sparrows that would be; what a picture of loneliness and sadness, as he sat perched upon the ridge of the splendid palace—with a magnificent home, indeed, but miserable for all that. I have sometimes asked myself if the Emperor Napoleon, in his superb palace, and his solitary greatness, ever feels "like a sparrow alone upon the house-top." David, it seems, did so.

So you see the little birds set me thinking about words in the dear Bible, and about God's precious promises, and about whether, after all, it may not be better to be little than to be great. But the peculiarly pleasant thought always was, "God feedeth them." The man or the child who gave them the crumbs they loved so well did not think of it, I dare say, but God, all the same, was using them to feed his little birds. God loves the tiny creatures, and takes care of them; not on account of their beauty, for the sparrow is not beautiful, but of a very plain, gray color; not because of their pretty song, for the sparrow cannot sing, but has only a kind of cheerful chirp; not because men set any great value upon them, for "are not five sparrows sold for two farthings?" It is because they are creatures he has made, and so made that they are capable of being happy, and it pleases him when he can see all such happy, and grieves him when, either by their own fault or the fault of others, they become miserable.

So these little birds live in their pretty home in perfect safety. No rude boy ever dares to throw a stone at them; no sportsman with his gun ever comes near them; they are surrounded by danger, yet always safe; for God keeps them and God feeds them.

Now I wish to show you, in one or two little stories, very simple, but very true, how faithful our Heavenly Father is in fulfilling those promises of which I have been speaking, and what wonderful ways he chooses in doing so. About twelve years ago, an English lady came one day into this same garden of the Tuileries, and sat down upon one of the many chairs placed there. I do not know whether the birds were there then, or not; but I think it doubtful. While she sat resting, she noticed that a gentleman with a little boy was occupying a seat very near her. The gentleman had been reading a little book which the boy now held in his hand. After a little he dropped it, and as he picked it up, she noticed that it was a French Testament. Immediately she said to the gentleman:

"I conclude that you love to read this little book."

"Yes," was his reply, "more than all others."

This led to a conversation, in which she learned that he had been, until very recently, a colporteur connected with the French Baptist mission in the city, and that he was a member of the mission church; that through deficiency of funds, the society in America, the Missionary Union, by which the mission was sustained, was unable longer to pay his salary, so that he had now no support for his family, and he feared that he must abandon his work. He told her what that work was; visiting every part of Paris, seeking out opportunities to do good, to enlighten his Catholic countrymen, and convince them how much better it is to trust in Jesus than in priests and masses.

The lady became so much interested that she determined to help him in this work. She was not a Baptist, but a very warm-hearted Christian, and one who had great faith in God. She was just on the point of returning to England, and she said to him, as they parted, that he must go right on as he had been doing, and that when she reached England she felt sure God would enable her to raise money to sustain him at least for a time. She had been a teacher. So she interested her former pupils and their parents in this good brother, and soon had secured money enough to pay his expenses for a month. This she sent him, with directions to keep on in his work and she would soon send him more. Twelve years have since passed. He has continued in his beloved service for Jesus and has never lacked. By means of this lady, and of friends raised up by her influence and that of others, sufficient money has always been provided. They do not take pains to solicit money; but they pray, as does he himself also, with faith in God, that the "daily bread" of the beloved colporteur may be given: and it comes, often in ways quite unexpected.

This excellent brother left my room only two or three hours since, after a very delightful visit. His name is Mr. Vignal. Don't you think that his three little children are God's sparrows; and does not God feed them?

UNCLE JOHN.

LETTER TENTH

THE BIRDS IN THE PALACE GARDEN.—CONCLUDED.

Dear Boys and Girls:

ANOTHER story I will tell you. Near this great city of Paris lives a rich Russian nobleman. His name is Prince Demidoff. He is immensely wealthy; has great estates and gold mines in Russia, and palaces, I don't know how many, in France and Italy. But he is a worldly, selfish man, and seems to care for nothing but his dogs and monkeys. He has a nephew, Count Demidoff, who is his heir. The Count is also very rich, and a few years ago was as worldly as his uncle, and a wild and wicked young man. But see by what wonderful means

God led him to think of and prefer the "more excellent way."

The nobility of Russia, like everybody else there, must always do just as the Emperor says. Over the higher nobles, especially, he seems to keep a very strict watch, even to choosing wives for them when they marry, and they must always marry the one he selects. A few years ago the young Count Demidoff was called home to St. Petersburg, from Paris, to marry a lady whom the Emperor had chosen for him. He had never seen her, and of course made her his wife simply because the Emperor commanded him to do so. But she was both beautiful and good, and very soon he loved her so much that when, at the end of a year, she died, his grief made him almost insane.

While in this sad state of mind he came again to Paris, and made the acquaintance here of an English nobleman named Lord Radstock, a warm-hearted Christian who, though a nobleman, and wealthy, devotes his life to doing good, and to leading men to the Saviour. We heard him preach, a few Sabbaths since, a plain, good, sweet gospel sermon. By Lord Radstock's means Count Demidoff was made to know Jesus. He found comfort at the foot of the cross, and now he lives to do good.

One of the Count's benevolent works I must tell you of. He has built, in one part of the city of Paris, a very large building, in which work is provided for poor, unemployed women, to the number of five hundred, with or without families. They come there every day; if they have children, they bring these with them; if any of the children are very small, they are put in charge of persons who take care of them while the mothers are at work. The larger ones go into a school in the same building, where they remain through the day. At evening, as the mother with her little flock passes out of the door to go home, she receives two francs, about forty cents, in money, and something, I believe, also, for each of the children.

Are not these children, and their mothers too, God's sparrows; and is it not very wonderful how he has provided for them? His providences towards Count Demidoff were not simply that he might become a Christian, but that he might be made an instrument to feed and comfort God's suffering poor.

And this leads me to ask myself whether God does not expect like things, more or less, of all to whom he has given any means of usefulness whatever. Are you and I, dear children, I wonder, feeding God's sparrows, in any way? I doubt if there is any one of us who can not do it at some time, and in some way, though ever so simple and humble. Let me tell you something I was reading of the other day.

At a certain place, here in France, there is a group of benevolent institutions called asylums. They have received very appropriate names. One is called "The Gospel Family;" another, "Bethesda;" another, "Ebenezer;" and the fourth, "Siloam-Bethel." The first is for young girls who have no one to take care of them, and who would run in the streets and be ruined, if neglected. They have a home here, are educated, learn to work, and when old enough are furnished with good places. The second is for young girls who are sick and friendless, for such as are blind, and for idiots. The third is for girls and boys subject to epileptic fits, and who, like the others, have none to take care of them. The fourth is for boys affected in any of the ways just described.

In the Bethesda asylum, not long ago, there was a poor idiot girl, named Celina. She could not speak, and could be taught almost nothing. But she had a sweet, pleasant temper, so that everybody loved her, and she was made to comprehend so much of religious truth as that there is a beautiful heaven, where all are happy. Her favorite employment was to sit by the bedside of the sick and drive away the flies, or make lint and roll up bands of linen for the infirmary.

After a time Celina was herself sick and died — died, as they said, with a smile upon her lips. What struck me most, in the narrative, were these words, by the person who relates it. He says:

"If the Lord asks of her, 'Celina, what have you done for me?' Celina can answer, 'I have driven away the flies from the poor sick, and I have made lint and rolled up bandages.'"

I thought, how many there are, with abundant gifts of mind of which poor Celina had almost none, and ample other means of usefulness, who have never done even so much as she in feeding God's sparrows.

But I must not make my letter too long; and yet I cannot well close without telling you a little how some of these things that I have been saying have applied to Aunt Esther and myself. About two months since, very shortly before the severe and long sickness from which she has not quite recovered, and which has left me feeble, almost, as a child, we were sitting late one evening by our cosy fire, and talking about the goodness of our Heavenly Father, of which the chapter, I think, which we had just been reading, reminded us; how he had taken care of us in our journey, and made everything so pleasant and easy for us. Then we said to one another, that perhaps trouble would come, sickness, or some other trial; but if it did, we added, we would *remember the birds in the palace garden*, for we had noticed the little creatures often, and thought and spoken of the fact that God cares for them, and much more for us.

Very soon after the sickness came; first Aunt Esther, with an infectious and most trying disorder, then a week later myself, with what at first was thought to be the same, but proved to be something else. Even the servants in the hotel were now afraid to come near us, and for a time we were almost without attendance, none of our friends venturing to visit us. But God remembered us, his poor wounded sparrows. He sent us soon the skillful physician and the kind nurses, and blessed what they did for us, so that though one of us has been so near the gate of death as to see its stern shape and the light beyond, we are both living, and hope soon to be both well.

During these tedious, lonely weeks, we have occasionally said to one another, "Remember the birds in the palace garden;" and they themselves have seemed to say the same. For, as our hotel is near the garden, they used to come occasionally and perch upon the little stone balconies outside our windows, where we could see them as we lay in bed, and would look in upon us, as if to say, "God takes care of us, and he will take care of you."

Ah, it is so good, dear children, to trust in God; to be able to come to him, in the name of Jesus, feeling sure that for that dear name's sake he has forgiven our sins and made us his sons and daughters. If you thus make him your own God and Father, as you may, in your happy youth, he will be your God and your keeper all the years of your life — will comfort you when sorrow comes, and when it is death, will save you in his own happy heaven. Remember, dear children, and you, older friends, who may read what I write, remember the birds in the palace garden.

UNCLE JOHN.

LETTER ELEVENTH.

THE OLD SOLDIERS AND THEIR GENERAL.*

Dear Boys and Girls:

WE went one day to visit the tomb of Napoleon the First, in Paris. It is one of the most interesting structures of that renowned city. Built in connection with the Hotel des Invalides, it occupies a space equal to a block of buildings in one of our cities. The tomb is on one side of a square, and the Hotel des Invalides on the three others, thus making a court-yard, in the centre of which is a spacious church for the invalid soldiers to worship in. For "Invalides" means invalid,

---

* I think it only fair to let the children know that this letter was written by Aunt Esther. — Uncle John.

that is, crippled, sick soldiers, or those infirm through age; and by "Hotel" is meant, not what you mean in America by that word, but an asylum or hospital.

The church I mentioned has a stone pavement made of little blocks of colored marble. We attended a service there one Sabbath. There were no seats except by the altar, the place where the priests officiate — for this, of course, is a Catholic church — and the vast area was filled with a motley group of soldiers, maimed and sick; some reclining upon movable couches, some sitting on sedan chairs; some stood, leaning upon crutches; some were armless, some eyeless. The visitors also had to stand. The arched ceiling is painted with battle scenes, and more than a hundred torn and battered flags, captured from enemies, hung there. Each of these flags had been carried in some terrible battle; some of them, perhaps, had been captured by some of these old soldiers, and dearly did they love to look at them, as signs of victory. If I could have seen somewhere a banner of the cross, which had won a victory over their hearts, and caused them to shout, "All hail, victorious Jesus!" I could have worshiped there with them. As you are American boys and girls, you may like to know that there were no stars and stripes among those captured flags.

The organ, during the service, responded occasionally to a chorus of drums played by little boys. When we left the church these drummer-boys went first, then the invalid soldiers, then the visitors. Everything was done in perfect order, and the reverential attitude of the worshipers, and their silent devotion, made it seem a solemn place.

The Hotel des Invalides, as I told you, is the home of these soldiers. It was built for this purpose by a great king, Louis the Fourteenth, just two hundred years ago, in 1670. The buildings and courts, all together, cover sixteen acres of ground, and there is accommodation for *five thousand* of these battered veterans. I went through the long corridors inside, and 'looked at the dormitories, or sleeping-places, which they occupy. Outside there is a balcony for them to walk in, and a garden of beautiful flowers for them to look at, or to cultivate. The kitchen and dining-rooms interested us very much. Food is prepared here for the sick, while those who have lost a leg, or an arm, only, and are not infirm, are supplied with a loaf of bread and a bottle of wine each day, with a little money, which they can spend as they please. I think the French know how to make good soldiers, by caring for them when they have thus become unable to march and fight, or even, perhaps, to work for a livelihood.

The tomb of Napoleon the First is a grand structure. I will try to give you some idea of it. An iron fence twenty feet high, with a soldier at each of the gates, guards the entrance. Passing through one of these gates, after a walk of a few rods, we went up a flight of marble steps, and were received by the attendant at the arched door into a magnificent circle, over which rose the lofty and splendid dome. This dome is filled with gorgeously painted windows, through which the light, changed to all the hues of the rainbow, falls down upon the place where the great Emperor sleeps. This immense dome is also gilded outside, so is the spire that rises from it to the height of more than three hundred feet from the ground, and when the sun is shining brightly it is splendid, and unlike anything else seen even in Paris.

We proceeded to the marble railing around the wide and deep basin containing the catafalque, or tomb proper. This catafalque is a full story below where we stood. It is made of granite from the island of Corsica, where Napoleon was born, and has upon the top of it a sarcophagus, or coffin — though not in the shape of a coffin, but of a large chest, with scroll-work at the ends. This is of Russia stone, which resembles mahogany. In this the Emperor lies, the place of his head being known only by the bouquets and wreaths of flowers placed there by those who love his memory. Near by is an altar, at which service is performed at five o'clock every morning. Around the catafalque are twenty-four statues in niches. The floor is mosaic, that is, made of blocks of colored marble. These are so shaped and arranged as to make twenty-four triangles, the points of which meet under the tomb, while at the broad end or base of each stands one of the statues. As I stood there and looked upon the artistic wonders of the place, I thought how much this Emperor is still beloved; and here, now,

"He sleeps his last sleep, he has fought his last
 battle;
No sound can awake him to glory again."

There are at the sides of this great room, the centre of which is occupied by the basin, or crypt, I have described, several chapels, in one of which are deposited the remains of Joseph, in another of Jerome, in another of Lucien Bonaparte. These were all brothers of the Emperor. Louis Napoleon, I suppose, expects some day to occupy one of them. We went down a flight of white marble stairs to the entrance of the crypt, or basin, where the Emperor lies. This entrance, with great, bronze doors, is permanently closed — sealed forever. No mortal man must lie beside the Emperor. Two of the generals he loved best, General Bertrand and General Duroc, are placed near the entrance; but within, he lies alone in his glory. Over the entrance the following sentence, taken from his will, is cut in the solid stone:

"I wish that my ashes may repose upon the banks of the Seine, in the midst of the people I have loved so much."

The wish has been granted. From the island of St. Helena, where he died, twenty years after his burial there, he was brought here, and this magnificent tomb assigned him by the French people, to show how much they adore the memory of Napoleon the First.

There will be something more about this in the next letter.

UNCLE JOHN.

LETTER TWELFTH.

HOW THE GENERAL CAME HOME.

Dear Boys and Girls:

THE Emperor Napoleon, after he had been defeated at Waterloo, in that terrible battle where the English Duke of Wellington commanded on one side and he upon the other, surrendered himself to the British, and by them was carried as a prisoner to the island of St. Helena, in the Atlantic ocean. Here he arrived on the 15th of October, 1815. Five years after he died, having remained a prisoner during all that time; not shut up in a gloomy building, it is true, as prisoners generally are, but still not allowed to leave the island. He was discontented and unhappy; not so great a man in *suffering* as he was in *acting*. Indeed, it is in suffering that it is always hardest of all for men to be very great. Jesus was so, was he not?

After Napoleon had remained buried in St. Helena twenty years, the French nation remembered what he had written in his will — that he wished to lie upon the banks of the Seine, in the midst of the people whom he loved. So they began to ask, "Is it not time for us to bring the great Emperor and General home?" Louis Philippe was the King of France at that time, and though he was not in any way related to the family of the Bonapartes, still he was interested, like the rest, in carrying out what Napoleon had wished so much. The island of St. Helena, however, belonged to England, and the French could not go upon the island and take up the body and bring it away without permission of the English Government. So King Louis inquired of the English if they were willing. They said they were; they thought it was a thing very proper to do, and they would be glad to see it done.

Accordingly, upon the 15th day of October, 1840, the same day of the year on which Napoleon had arrived at St. Helena, and twenty years after his burial there, two splendid French ships of war sailed from Havre, the sea-port at the mouth of the Seine, one hundred miles from Paris, to bring the General and the Emperor home. The ships were commanded by Prince de Joinville, a son of the King, Louis Philippe. In three weeks he arrived at St. Helena, and, accompanied by the Governor of the island and other official persons, he went to the spot, in a lovely little valley, where the temporary tomb of Napoleon had been made. They opened it and found the coffin just as it had been placed there, twenty years before. There was first a coffin of mahogany; in this was one of lead, and in this another of tin. In the tin coffin the body lay. It had been kept so closely shut from the air that when they opened the coffin, they found the face of the Emperor very little changed, so that those who had seen him in life recognized it in a moment. It was a solemn, affecting time.

The coffins were then closed as before, and carried to the ships, a long procession accompanying, in which nearly all the people on the island joined. The ships then sailed for France, and when they arrived at Havre again the coffins were taken on board a smaller ship, one that could sail up the Seine to Paris. There was a very splendid catafalque prepared on deck on which to put them, and at night there were lights so placed as to shine directly upon it and make it gleam and glitter as if covered with brilliant stars. All along the Seine, between Havre and Paris, there are cities and villages. At these the people would come out to meet the funeral ship, as it drew near, with processions and solemn music. They built arches of flowers over the river, under which the ship would pass, while its decks were covered with the bouquets and garlands they placed there.

At last the ship reached Paris. There it was met by some great persons whom the King had sent for the purpose; the catafalque was taken from it and carried through the streets to the Place de la Concorde. Here the King met it, and the Prince de Joinville said,

"Sire, I present to you the body of the Emperor Napoleon."

The King replied, "I receive it in the name of France."

He then gave to Marshal Soult, who had been one of the greatest of Napoleon's generals, the sword which Napoleon had carried in leading the great armies he commanded, and said to him, "General, I charge you to place this sword of the Emperor upon his coffin."

This was done, and the procession moved on. When it arrived at the Hotel des Invalides, the coffins were taken from the catafalque and the funeral car, and by thirty-two of Napoleon's Old Guard, soldiers who had marched and fought with him in many a hard campaign up to Waterloo, carried into the church. In the esplanade, before the Hotel des Invalides, there were not less than thirty thousand people; and in the porticoes within, surrounding the court through which the procession would pass to the tomb, six thousand more. After service in the church, the body was carried to the tomb, and placed as described in the last letter. And this is how the General came home.

Now, Napoleon was, doubtless, a very great man. I shall not say that the honors paid to his memory are more than he deserved, for I think that nations ought to honor their rulers, and while Napoleon did very wrong in bringing on so many wars, and was influenced in what he did far too much by his love of power and of praise, still he was the means of great good to France. I am glad, too, that he lies now where he wished to lie — at home, not in that lonely island; among the people he loved, not in the soil of the stranger and the enemy.

But I cannot help thinking how differently Jesus — who Napoleon himself said was far greater than he, or than Cæsar, or than Alexander, or any of the great men of this world — desires to have us show our love, from that way in which the French show their love for their Emperor. He does not require us to build monuments to him. It is true he *needs* no tomb, for his body rose from the tomb where it was laid and ascended, glorified, into heaven. But neither does he require any thing of the kind. You remember, do you not, how he said we must show our love to him? — by loving each other, and being kind to the poor and the perishing — by seeking, as he did, to save the lost.

At the same time, there was something in the sight of those old soldiers at the Invalides which made me think of what every Christian should be. If we only loved our Great Captain as they loved theirs! How proud and glad they felt to be known as his soldiers! What a sacred, happy place to them was the spot where they knew his body is laid! Though so poor, so old, so feeble, so maimed, some of them, they would not have changed places with the young Prince Imperial, son of the Emperor, over at the Tuileries; it was better to have been a soldier of the Great Napoleon, than to be young, and rich, and the heir to a throne. Ah, it is much more to be a Christian!

Then, *our* General is coming home again some day. Not as Napoleon came; — more gloriously even than they brought him; and not sleeping in a coffin unmindful of all that is done in his honor. He will come as the Living Redeemer; come with the angels attending, and not riding in ships, or in funeral cars, but in chariots of salvation. He will come, not to be housed in a tomb, as Napoleon is, however gorgeously, but to open the tombs with the word of his mouth, and to call up the sleeping saints to meet their Lord in the air.

Oh, let me be a soldier of Jesus. Let me be one of those who shall welcome him when he comes again "to be admired in all them that believe," to take unto him his kingdom in final triumph, and reign forever and ever.

UNCLE JOHN.

LETTER THIRTEENTH.

THE STORY OF A CASTLE.

Dear Boys and Girls:

SOME time ago I told you " the story of a king." Would you like to read, now, " the story of a castle?" Please, then, to take your maps and find near the southern coast of England the Isle of Wight. Imagine yourselves, next, just about in the middle of this beautiful island, and that you have climbed the high hill which you saw rising from the midst of a lovely valley as you rode over from Ryde yonder, opposite Portsmouth, with Aunt Esther and me. You have not only climbed the hill, but have now clambered also to the top of a gray old wall, very high and very ancient, from which you are looking out upon one of the most charming landscapes, I will venture to say, you ever saw. It is not grand, like some of our American ones, except in the wide sweep of country which the eye takes in, and which, to your right and left, as you stand looking northward, reaches from sea to sea. Just at your feet is a small village, with its ancient church hundreds of years old; a little farther away is another and larger village; both are embowered in fine old trees, while each has its small stream which winds away through the valley, a gleam of silver amid the green fields. In the still farther distance, on every side, you see the rich lands of the "Garden Isle," as they appropriately call it; the gently swelling hills crowned with trees, the green slopes and valleys, the cottages of the poor and the mansions of the rich; while far away yonder are the towers of a queen's palace — Osborne House, one of the favorite homes of Queen Victoria. Where could you find a lovelier scene? This old castle to whose battlements we have climbed is Carisbrooke Castle; the nearer and smaller of the two villages down there is the village of Carisbrooke, and the one farther away is Newport, the capital of the island. It is this castle, mostly in ruins now, whose "story," at least some part of it, I wish to tell you.

I suppose that if we were to "begin at the beginning" of our story we should have to go back almost to the very time, so long ago, when our Saviour lived upon the earth. Before that time, even, more than eighteen hundred and seventy years since, as nearly as can be made out, the people who first inhabited this island found it lying here like a gem in the sea. They came over to it, either from Britain — as it then was, England now — or from the coast of France, to the southward yonder. They were not exactly the same sort of people that live on the island now, but differed from them very nearly the same as a Welshman differs from an Englishman. One of the earliest places they occupied was this little village, here at the foot of the hill. Here they built their small huts with roofs shaped like a sugar-loaf, and lived no doubt by fishing in this stream below which seems then to have been quite a large river; and because their village was thus built upon the river bank, they called it Carisbrooke, which in their language meant "the town on the stream." It bewilders us to think, as you and I stand here upon the old wall of the castle and look down upon the village roofs, how very long ago that must have been.

It was the custom of the people of whom I am telling you, when they built a town, especially one which they expected to make an important one, to build also some kind of a fortress or fort near it, for defense against their enemies. So it appears that those who first settled here at Carisbrooke, noticing the high and rugged hill near them, rising up out of the valley, and in some places quite difficult of ascent, saw that it was a good place for a fort, and accordingly built one upon the summit, in their own rude fashion. This was the beginning of Carisbrooke Castle. The people I speak of were Britons, not such as Englishmen and Americans now are, for they are Saxon in their origin, but such as the inhabitants of Wales, or the Welshmen are. About as long ago as when our Saviour was living on the earth, it is thought that they first inhabited the village of Carisbrooke, and began, in their rude way, this castle on the hill.

Some five hundred years after, the Saxons came. We will now go down from this part of the wall where we have been standing, and crossing the castle-yard into the northeast corner of it, we see rising above us a round tower, covered to the very top with ivy. A long flight of stone steps, eighty-one in number, will lead us to the summit, and, if you please, we will ascend them. You perceive that there is no way of getting into the tower but by those steps; and if you observe closely you will see that the tower itself is built upon the summit of a high mound, which seems to have been thrown up for the purpose, and the sides of which are now covered with small trees and shrubs. Along the slope of this mound the stone steps run until they bring you to the gates of the tower. Of these gates you see that there were three, and some of the iron hinges on which they hung are still in the wall. The first of the gates was what is called a portcullis, that is a strong heavy gate, moving up and down in grooves, and with sharp iron spikes along the lower edge. You can see now the grooves in the stone pillars on each side the gate-way. Beyond this there are two other gates, and then you come into the tower, now an open space, the roof having long since decayed. You perceive that an enemy wishing to take this tower would have first to come up those steep stone stairs, then force his way through those three gates, with the defenders shooting at him from the loop-holes and from the summit. The only possible way to take it would be to batter it down, which would be easy enough in these days, but would have been impossible in those when the tower was built, for then they had no cannon for such purposes. This tower was called "The Keep," because it was so strong. It was built by the Saxons, probably not less than thirteen hundred years ago.

But now our "story" comes forward five hundred years more, and we are at the time when William the Conqueror crossed over from France, and in the dreadful battle of Hastings made himself master of England. He and those who came over with him were called Normans, because they lived in Normandy, a part of France. A few days ago I stood upon that old battle-ground. I saw where the Normans and the Saxons fought each other, with their terrible weapons, from seven in the morning until night, and the spot where Harold, then the King of England, fell, with an arrow in his brain. Among those who came over with William was a nobleman named Fitz-Osborne. To him the king gave Carisbrooke Castle, with the village and broad lands adjacent. He built these other walls which we see around us; the massive gateway, also, through which we passed as we entered the castle, the chapel of St. Nicholas, whose ruined wall we saw upon our right as we came in, the mansion for the residence of the governor or captain of the castle which we saw in front, and all these high, strong walls, which enclose about an acre and a half of ground. All these were built by William Fitz-Osborne, not far from eight hundred years ago.

If, now, we come forward again another five hundred years, we are in the time of Elizabeth, the great Queen. By that time the castle needed repairing. She repaired it, and also enlarged it. You remember that as we came up the hill, we left by mistake the direct road to the entrance of the castle and went round to the back of it. We were thus obliged to almost encircle it before reaching the only place where a visitor can get in. We thought it a long walk; — and so it was, much longer than if the castle were now as Fitz-Osborne left it, for Elizabeth caused extensive out-works, as they are called, to be built; — that is, another strong wall, though not so high, with embankments of earth within, upon which cannon could be planted. These additional walls makes the whole space enclosed about twenty acres. No wonder we felt tired when at the end of such a long walk, after climbing the steep hill, besides. But we reached the entrance at last, and there we found more of Elizabeth's work. For before we came, in entering, to the main wall and gate, we had to pass through another one, and then along a winding passage, with a wall on either side of us. These, too, were built by Elizabeth, about three hundred years ago. Since then the castle has remained as it now is, except that after some time less care was shown in preserving it, and little by little it has fallen in ruins, with the exception of the exterior walls and the mansion house within.

Connected with the mansion house, or near it, is a very curious thing — the well-house.

This is a small stone building within which is a well *two hundred and forty feet deep*. It is one hundred and fifty feet down to the water, which itself has a depth of ninety feet. Of course it would be impossible to bring up water from such a depth by hand, so they have a large wheel, to which a horizontal beam is attached running over the top of the well, with a strong rope winding around it. The wheel is worked by a donkey. At the command of his master he gets upon the inside of the rim of the wheel, at the bottom, of course. This rim is about three feet wide, and as he treads it the wheel turns round, the beam turns also and winds up the rope, and, slowly, up comes the big bucket, filled with water wonderfully sweet and cool. Not long ago a donkey died here which had worked in this wheel for forty years, and the one before him had done duty in the same way for forty-five years. The well, the wall of which is amazingly strong, was built in the time of King Stephen, or about seven hundred years ago; the wheel and beam now in use were put there in the time of Elizabeth.

But, that I may not make my letter too long,

I will stop here, now, and tell you in my next about some of the people who have lived in the castle.

UNCLE JOHN.

LETTER FOURTEENTH.

THE STORY OF A CASTLE — CONCLUDED.

Dear Boys and Girls:

IT is wonderful to think what a busy, bustling scene Carisbrooke Castle once presented, still and melancholy as it is now. Through the great gate-way by which we entered, how often have bands of steel-clad soldiers marched in; how many times have warrior-knights, in glittering armor, with their banners and trumpets, and their scores of followers, pranced through; how often more peaceful processions, splendid groups of ladies and gentlemen returning from the chase, gaily chattering as they passed under the massive arch and came out into the castle-yard, where, perhaps, little children, boys and girls, were at play.

At other times the soldiers, mounting the walls, have seen their enemy encamped below, and have manfully resisted them. But, although several times besieged, the old castle was never taken.

One part of our story is a sad one. Have you ever read of the Civil Wars in England; those, I mean, between King Charles the First and his Parliament? You may remember how trouble arose between them which grew at last into a war; how several battles were fought, and how, at last, the King was defeated and made prisoner. He was kept, at first, in a kind of honorable captivity at Hampton Court, a palace near London. From this, however, he escaped, and after concealing himself for a while at a place where the people were friendly to him, it occurred to him that he would try to have the Governor of Carisbrooke Castle, one Colonel Hammond, give him a shelter here. It ended in his being brought to the castle as a prisoner. When a boy of nine years, and again when a youth of eighteen, he had been here, and had gone out and come in with hunting parties, such as I spoke of a minute ago. Over yonder, in what was then Parkhurst Forest, but where you now see those extensive barracks for soldiers, he went hunting, and as he returned to the castle little dreamed, I suppose, that it was one day to be his prison. And yet, thirty years after the second of those visits, he rode up again along the path that now winds so beautifully under the trees, rounding the hill, and, with the stern Puritan soldiers guarding him, passed in by the gateway, which then, no doubt, seemed to him gloomy and threatening.

At first the prisoner-king was treated well, but, little by little, things changed. One after another of his old servants were sent away, until at last his best friend near him was an old man who came in each morning to light his fire. His hair and beard turned gray and grew to a great length, while his clothes were neglected and soon became very unlike what kings are wont to wear. Twice he tried to escape, each time by a window in the castle. The first time the opening between the bars was too small, and after passing his head through he hung by the breast and shoulders until, with much difficulty, he succeeded in forcing himself back. He was then removed to another part of the castle, and after some time made another attempt. One of the window-bars he cut in two with a file and some aqua fortis which friends outside had managed to send in to him. But just as he was passing out through the wider opening so made, he saw that men were on guard under the window, and that escape was thus made impossible. Sadly he closed his window and went back to his bed.

After many months had thus passed, the Parliament proposed terms of agreement; the king was taken from the castle down to Newport, that he might meet the messengers sent to confer with him. Terms were finally agreed to, but meanwhile the army, which was unfriendly to Charles, had got the power in its hands, and by its means the king was taken away as a prisoner to another castle where he remained until they took him to London and put him to death. In the register of the old church at Carisbrooke there are two records made, which tell, in a few sad words, how this sorrowful history ended. The first is:

7*

"The sixth day of September, King Charles went from the Castle to Newport to treat, and the last day of November he went from Newport to Hurst Castle to prison, carried away by two troops of horse."

The second is as follows:

"In the year of our Lord 1649. January the 30th day, was King Charles beheaded at Whitehall Gate."

It was in 1647 that he had been first taken to Carisbrooke Castle, and so from that time till his death not far from two years must have elapsed. As we entered the castle through the main gate, did you notice a large window in the wall upon the left hand? It is in what must have been the second story of the rooms which then ran along upon that side, and the ruins of which you now see at the base of the wall. That window is the one by which King Charles tried the second time to escape. You see that it has iron bars running up and down it, half as thick as a man's wrist. One of these bars has been taken out. I wonder if it is the one which King Charles cut with his file and his aqua fortis.

There is another window, still more sadly associated with the history of this same king, which I could show you if you would visit London with me some time. As we rode down from Trafalgar Square, where the monument to Lord Nelson, the great sailor, is, to Westminster Abbey, we should pass through what used to be the inner court of the palace of Whitehall, but is now a street. A part of the palace is still standing, and at one corner of the second story is the window out of which the king stepped upon the scaffold which had been built close to it, and a few minutes after laid his head upon the executioner's block. These two windows, in Carisbrooke Castle and in the Palace of Whitehall, will be memorable for a long time, will they not?

But there is still another person of whom I must speak to you in this Story of a Castle. This time it is a little girl. When she comes to live in the castle she is only in her fifteenth year. She is a king's daughter. Perhaps you sometimes think that it must be very nice to be the son or daughter of a king, and that such can never have many things to trouble them, but everything possible to make them happy. This little girl had trouble enough, though she was, in spite of that, a cheerful and happy child. Her name was Elizabeth, and she was the daughter of the king of whom I just spoke to you, King Charles the First. About a year and a half after her father's death she was brought to Carisbrooke Castle, with her brother Henry, two years younger. The persons who then governed England did not wish that there should be any more kings or queens in that country, and since these children of King Charles might some day wish to be such, or some people might try to make them such, they shut them up in this castle. They were allowed to run about inside the castle, and to play upon the green in the castle yard, but not to go outside the walls; so they, too, were prisoners.

But Elizabeth did not remain long a prisoner. In less than a month she died. She had always had poor health, and the confinement now, with the sorrow she had felt at her father's sad fate, made her much worse, so that she soon died. But she died very happy. Her father, shortly before his death, had given her a Bible as a keepsake. This, when she was dying, she asked those who waited upon her to place under her head. It was thus seen how much she loved her father, but I think, also, how much she loved the dear Book of God. Many things that she said, too, showed that she loved and trusted in the Saviour, and when she died, I have no doubt, her soul, from the castle-prison, went to be free and happy in heaven.

They buried her in a church in Newport, of which I spoke in my former letter as now the capital of the island. This was more than two hundred years ago. It was forgotten after a time that she had been buried there, as there was nothing placed over the spot to keep it in memory. But a few years since, when some workmen were digging a grave for some other person, they found a lead coffin with the inscription, "Elizabeth, second daughter of King Charles the First, who died at Carisbrooke Castle, Sept. 8th, 1650." Of course they did not disturb it, but covered it again and placed another inscription where it could be seen, directly over the spot. In 1856, a little more than two hundred years after the death of the young princess, Queen Victoria caused a monument to be placed in the church, the marble figure of a young girl lying with her head upon a Bible. Upon the monument are these words:

"*To the memory of the Princess Elizabeth, daughter of King Charles I., who died at Carisbrooke Castle, Sept. 8. 1650, and is interred beneath the chancel of this church, this monument is erected as a token of respect for her virtues and of sympathy for her misfortunes, by Victoria R.*"

This was a beautiful act in Queen Victoria, was it not? As we stood looking at the lovely marble figure, and thought of the long sickness and the long sorrow of this young princess, we felt glad that there is a heaven where the suffering and the sorrowful shall suffer and be sorrowful no more.

But now, as we have come down from the castle, I think I will take you with me to another place and tell you about another young person, not unlike the lovely and gentle Princess Elizabeth, although in a very different condition of life. Do you have among your Sabbath-school books the one entitled "Little Jane, the Young Cottager?" She was a dear little Christian girl, so good and so intelligent, although so

Little Jane Learning the Verses.

poor and with so few opportunities of improvement, that her pastor, Legh Richmond, wrote a book about her after her death. The church where he preached is at Brading, also in the Isle of Wight, and a few miles from Ryde. It is a very ancient church, having been built in the year 704, and is now more than eleven hundred and fifty years old. Just in the rear of it "Little Jane" is buried. We rode over to Brading on the evening of the day after our visit to Carisbrooke Castle, and saw the church, and the spot where little Jane lies. Upon the stone are these lines, written by the good minister who wrote the book:

> "Ye who the power of God delight to trace
> And mark with joy each monument of grace,
> Tread softly o'er this grave, as ye explore
> 'The short and simple annals of the poor.'
>
> "A child reposes underneath this sod,
> A child to memory dear, and dear to God.
> Rejoice, yet shed the sympathetic tear;
> Jane the 'Young Cottager' lies buried here."

It was the 30th of January, 1799, that little Jane died, at the age of fifteen. So long ago as that, children did not have such Sunday-school books, nor such Sunday-schools as we now have; and this little girl with others, young like herself, was sent into the church-yard often, and made to learn the pious verses on the tombstones, as one way of interesting them in sacred things. Little Jane was very willing to do this, and they show to visitors the stone from which she learned the verses that she liked best. I will copy them here:

" Forgive, blest shade, the tributary tear,
   That mourns thy exit from a world like this;
Forgive the wish that would have kept thee here,
   And stayed thy progress to the seats of bliss.

" No more confined to grovelling scenes of night,
   No more a tenant pent in mortal clay;
Now should we rather hail thy glorious flight,
   And trace thy journey to the realms of day."

Do you not think that little Jane and the Princess Elizabeth must have been somewhat alike, although one was a King's daughter and the other a cottager? True religion is just the same in the one as in the other, and the love of Jesus will show itself in just the same way in both. They both wear crowns now. They are in the happy world where there are no castles and no graves; for there men are never wicked and never try to kill each other, and there, too, "they die no more."

Uncle John.

LETTER FIFTEENTH.

A WALK BY A RIVER.

Dear Boys and Girls:

S I have written to you in former letters about things in England, France and Italy, it may be well to write one that shall tell you something of what I have seen in Scotland; these four which I have named being the countries I have visited, chiefly, while abroad. So I am going to write to you about "A Walk by a River."

The river is a very small one. In fact, it can scarcely, with propriety, be called a river at all. It is more like what the Scotch people call, I believe, a "burn," or brook. And as it is a "burn" full of little rapids and waterfalls, **a**

still more suitable name, at least in this part of it, would be a "linn," which means a waterfall. The name of the stream is the Eske, but the particular locality I am to describe is called Roslin; I suppose because "linn" meaning a waterfall, and "ross" a promontory or cliff, and as this little stream, or succession of rapids and cascades, runs between high cliffs, in some places covered with trees, in others mere naked rocks, the word "Roslin" would tell exactly what it is. The walk which I took is about one mile in length, descending to the little river at one end from the cliffs, and then at the other climbing up to their top again.

I will begin my little story where I began my walk. After riding in the cars about seven miles south of Edinburgh, I got out at a station called Hawthornden; that is, "the den of hawthorns"—the hawthorn being, as you know, the tough and sturdy little tree, or shrub, which the people in England and Scotland make hedges of, instead of fences, for their farms. But there are a good many nice things growing around and in Hawthornden, besides the hawthorn. After walking about a quarter of a mile from the station, I turned in at a gate through a solid stone wall, and found myself at once in one of the most lovely parks I have seen anywhere. It was not level, as many parks are, but broken into little hills and slopes, along which the path wound downward to the "den," under noble elms and oaks, while the green sward on each side was smooth, and bright, and clean as possible. It was hard to "keep off the grass," as the notice at the gate told me to do. After winding downward along this path for some time, with the views changing at almost every step, and each one with some new beauty in it, I came at last in sight of what seemed at first like the ruins of a castle; a high old wall, some day evidently part of a fine residence, but now standing roofless, and covered with ivy. A few steps further brought into view the whole building, a portion of which has been kept in repair, and is a commodious dwelling.

This was the house to which the name Hawthornden had been given, because built, as you will see, in a kind of den where once, I suppose, if not now, the hawthorn was very abundant. Here, between two and three hundred years ago, a poet lived, named William Drummond, and his descendants are here still. He lived at the same time with Shakespeare, Ben Jonson, Queen Elizabeth, and some other of the great folks we read about. I can not stop now to tell you any more of him than just to mention a visit he had once from one of the persons I have mentioned, Ben Jonson. "Ben," as everybody called him, was himself a poet, and a writer of stage-plays; not so good a man as I wish he was, but quite a famous one in his day. When Ben arrived, Drummond, or "Hawthornden," as people often called him, sat in a pleasant seat under a large sycamore, which was still standing a few years ago. As he sat there, looking out for his guest, I presume, he saw a large, portly man coming down the walk, with a step as independent, and with as much an air of being at home as if the house and grounds belonged to him, and he were at home in reality. Drummond recognized him and called out,

"Welcome, welcome, royal Ben;"

and Ben replied, poet-like, with a rhyme,

"Thank ye, thank ye, Hawthornden."

They had a good time together, and Drummond afterwards made a book about it.

Visitors are not allowed to go into the house, but they may go *under* it. The house is built upon a high, rocky cliff, one of those I told you about just now. In ancient times, nobody knows when, some caves were cut in the solid rock of this cliff, and were then reached by some steps which had been also cut downward along the cliff, in a slanting direction, where it faces the ravine. There were twenty-seven of these steps running down from the top; at the foot of them was a little bridge crossing a chasm, and then there were eight more steps leading up to the entrance of the caves, a hole just about large enough to admit one person. This is as it used to be. The steps and the bridge, however, are now never used, but an opening into the caves has been made, so that they can be entered from the garden.

As you go in, you are first in a long, arched passage, seventy-five feet in length and six in breadth, which conducts you straight to the other side where the entrance used to be, and through which you look down into the glen, and hear the rippling of the stream below. Connected with this passage are three other rooms; one called "the King's bed-chamber," another "the "King's dining-room," and another "the King's guard-room." In one of these rooms the wall upon one side is cut out into little box-like compartments, each about nine inches square, which look as if they might have been meant for books, or as "pigeon-holes," for keeping papers and other things. They call this "the King's library." It is pretended that King Robert Bruce, a very famous man who lived a long while ago, made these caves his dwelling, at a time when his enemies had become too strong for him, and he was obliged to hide himself for a while. In the end of the long passage where you come near the ancient entrance there is what they call his broad-sword lying upon a table, along with the writing-desk of John Knox, the great Reformer in Queen Mary's time. I do not find that there is any history for what they say of Bruce having lived here, and I doubt if he ever did. The caves were probably made in the old stormy times, when people needed such places to hide in, or in which to keep their valuables from robbers. But it is time we had resumed our "walk by the river."

A little way from the house I have just been describing, the visitor leaves the handsome, garden-like grounds, and comes into what is still a wilderness. At first the path runs along the verge of the high cliff, and stepping a little to the right, one may look down the steep face of it, hundreds of feet into the deep ravine. Passing on from this, he descends in a path that winds about under the trees, which have been left to grow in their own wild way, catching here and there glimpses of the high, rocky walls of the glen. After a time the little river is reached and crossed by a wooden bridge, just wide enough for one person at a time. Near the end of the bridge a gate opens, and when you have passed, shuts and locks itself, so that it is impossible to return through it. Then along the river side you go, under the steep cliff, now up a few steps, now down again near the margin of the stream, now with a bare, frowning rock hanging over you, now with trees and shrubs clothing the less precipitous sides; everything is still save the singing of the stream as it swiftly courses over its stony bed, the whisper of the wind in the tree-tops, and now and then, perhaps, the carol of a bird. You seem out of the world, in that secluded place, and can scarcely believe that there are great and noisy cities, busy, bustling crowds, to which in a few moments you must go back.

I must not linger on my road, as I have something to tell you of at the end. Fancy yourselves, then, making your way for a mile, by a narrow path, through what, save for the path, is as much a wilderness still as when the human foot first entered it. After a while the trees begin to part; you look forward and there is more light; evidently you are coming out into an open country again. The cliff, on the side where you are walking, becomes a steep slope, instead of a precipice, and is covered with green grass instead of trees and underbrush. Upon the top is a church, gray with age, yet beautiful, with its gothic windows and pinnacles. Looking forward, you see the still grayer ruins of a castle, not quite so high up as the church, and partly hidden in trees. These are Roslin Castle and Roslin Chapel. Pursuing your way to the castle, you find it is a ruin indeed, with the exception of one building within the walls, which is still a dwelling.

We are here once more among the decaying works of men long since passed away. It is probably eight or nine hundred years since Roslin Castle was built, and the chapel is at least half as old. Wandering among the ruins of the former, as it " frowns o'er the rocky steep," you can scarcely believe that it was once what we are told it was. I find it said by one very old writer that the proud Scottish knight who lived in it some four hundred years ago, Sir William Sinclair, Prince of the Orkney Islands, was served at his table in vessels of gold and silver. He had one lord to superintend his household, another to give him his cup of wine at dinner, another to do his carving; while his lady was served by seventy-five gentlemen, and by fifty-three ladies all daughters of noblemen, adorned in silk and velvet, with chains of gold and all sorts of jewelry. When she rode out two hundred horsemen attended her, and if at night, eighty other men, with lighted torches. What a grand person, truly! Where are they all now? There is not an echo of voice or step on Roslin steep to-day to remind of the gay and busy scene of the times so long gone by, and the proud hall where they reveled and rejoiced has crumbled wholly away. Alas, what is human greatness? A dream only.

They tell a curious story of the man who owned and occupied Roslin Castle in the time of Robert Bruce. His name, I think, was Sir Oliver Sinclair. King Robert, who then lived in Edinburgh, was very fond of hunting, and used often to chase the deer on Pentland Hills, which are near to Roslin. He had several times started a deer of a peculiar color, so swift that his dogs had never succeeded in pulling her down. One day, as he was out as usual, accompanied by his knights and among them Sir Oliver Sinclair, he spoke of the deer, and in rather a bantering tone asked if any of them could succeed better than he. Sir Oliver had two dogs, one of them named "Help," and the other "Hold," which he asserted were better dogs than the King's, and would catch the deer. He offered at length to wager his head against a certain tract of land near by, called Pentland

Moor, that his dogs would catch the deer before she could cross a little stream named March burn. The deer was soon roused. Help and Hold pressed hard after her. The knight seemed likely to lose his wager and his life. They say that he called out,

"Help, Haud (Hold), an' ye may,
Or Roslin will lose his head this day."

The deer plunged into the burn, and was half way across, when Hold seized her, and Help coming quickly up, they together brought her down. Thus Sir Oliver won a handsome addition to his lands. But I have no idea, for my part, that if he had lost his wager, he would at the same time have lost his head. Perhaps the story is *only* a story. Anyhow, it has a lesson for us. Help and Hold are the right sort of dogs to do our hunting with in this world. We must "hold" hard if we mean to really win any prize, and be as ready to "help" as to hold. Only let us be sure that we hunt for right things, and in a right way.

But now, as our walk by the river is finished, I must tell you what it makes me think of. I think it is much like our walk through life. I can remember when life seemed to me very much as the park at Hawthornden seemed as I turned into it through the gate that bright afternoon; when it appeared a very pleasant thing to live, and as if there was not much else to do in this world but to run cheerily along a smooth path, with the green slopes around, and the whispering leaves overhead. That is where you are now, dear boys and girls, and perhaps you sometimes wonder at the wrinkles, and furrows, and gray hairs which we older ones bear, and are puzzled to understand why life should seem so hard. But the path soon leaves the park, with its walks and slopes and flower-beds. Before we know it we are amid the thickets of the wilderness. The steep cliff of which I spoke, upon whose dizzy verge I stood looking down into the gulf, is like the first great temptation which one encounters. As you approach, there seems no such abyss there. The ravine is narrow just at that point, and as you see the green branches on the other side, you imagine that you can, if you choose, go *down* the steep and then *up* again under those pleasant trees. But arrived at the verge, you perceive that there is no way to go down but to plunge headlong, while sure that to do this will be to be dashed in pieces. Happy they who recoil in season from the brink of the temptation that entices to ruin!

The path along the stream has something of the ruggedness and the changefulness of our way in life. The gate I spoke of, which opens to let us pass but admits of no return, is like that stern destiny which forbids us to go back, no matter what we may have lost by the way we have come, no matter what we may dread in the way we have yet to go. The voices of the stream, of the leaves, and of the birds, are like those kind voices with which a good Heavenly Father makes the air melodious as we go on, if only we have ears to hear them, and are not so impatient with the hardness of the way as to have no room in our minds for cheerful thoughts. At last, upon the high hills from which we see far over into the life beyond, we perceive around us ruins, indeed, many things broken and crumbled, many works come to naught, many hopes perishing; but, like the chapel on Roslin steep, Religion is there, also, to tell of a life where there are no ruins, and no foot-sore pilgrims like ourselves.

As I think of my walk by the river, I can understand better a good many things which I have known through life. But this I see — that so far as, earlier or later, I took any divine promise and held it in my hand as a guide along the rough way, as a help or a hope, it has been a promise never-failing. Let me assure you, dear young friends, that there are safe ways in life, though a thousand times more rough and trying than the path by Roslin Water, and that these are the ways in which the Good Father leads, as he holds us by the hand.

UNCLE JOHN.

LETTER SIXTEENTH.

TOM GROWLER AND HIS BROTHERS.

Dear Boys and Girls:

DO any of you happen to know who Tom Growler is? I dare say not; and I think you would never guess. You would be likely to first guess it is a boy, perhaps, then a dog, or a horse, or a lion. Tom Growler is none of these. Tom Growler is a *bell!* There! I knew you would be astonished. Yes, a bell, and a big one; and all his big brothers are bells. Of course Tom lives in a steeple. It is a London steeple, and the most famous one there; one of the steeples, or towers, of great St. Paul's — a cathedral or church large enough to hold inside of it four or five of the largest churches in Illinois. Tom Growler has had rather a curious history. His name used to be Great Tom of Westminster. One of the English poets, I forget who, put him once into a couplet, that is two lines of verse, which he wrote one night when he and some of his friends were out later than they ought to be:

"Hark! Harry, 'tis time to be gone,
 For Westminster Tom, by my faith, strikes one."

Tom hung, at the time when these lines were written — more than a hundred and fifty years ago — in a tower near Westminster Abbey, in London, which was called the Tower of Westminster. It stood at the entrance of a very large and stately building called Westminster Hall, through which one passes in going into the Houses of Parliament. The bell was used in connection with a clock for striking the hours, and to ring on great occasions. It was very old. While it hung in this Tower of Westminster it had a Latin inscription upon it, which I will quote, although, of course, you will not know what it means till I tell you. This is the inscription, some of the words being spelt a little differently from the way we spell the same words now:

> "Tercius aptavit me Rex, Edwardque vocavit,
> Sancti decore Edwardi signeretur ut hore."

The meaning is, that the Third King had placed it there, and named it Edward, that it might indicate the hours of Saint Edward, or be rung in honor and memory of Saint Edward. By "the Third King" is meant Henry III., king of England. "Saint Edward" is another English king who reigned some time before Henry, and is called Edward the Confessor. The inscription, then, tells us that the bell was made in Henry the Third's time and named Edward, after Edward the Confessor, that when it was rung it might be a memorial of him. This would be just about six hundred years ago.

Well, for about four hundred and fifty years Tom hung in the tower of Westminster, and did his duty there, without ever stopping to think that in that long interval he would have to tell the time of day about four million times. In 1708 they wanted him at St. Paul's, but in carrying him to the cathedral they cracked him, and he had to be melted down and made over. Out of this hot furnace, as people often do, he came bigger than ever, for they put in new supples of the stuff he was made of. So he came out a big fellow, and when they had got him fairly housed in the steeple, he began roaring out the time of day in such a mighty, booming voice, that they gave him a new name, and called him Tom Growler. I heard him once telling the world it was twelve o'clock, and I must say, if everybody would growl as musically as he goes, people might growl as much as they pleased, for aught I care.

Well, this is Tom Growler's history, told in a very few words, though he has *tolled* it in a very great many more, in his sort of language. Tom has four brothers, all of them younger than himself, I believe, and all having the same name. If they lived in the same family, this might cause some confusion. But it so happens that they do not live together, and so they can be distinguished by the names of the places they live in. One of them has taken Tom Growler's place at Westminster, though in a new and much handsomer tower. He is called Tom of

Westminster. I have heard him, too, sing out the time of day, and a wonderfully sweet voice he has. Another is at Oxford, and so is called Tom of Oxford. He lives in the tower of Christ Church College, in that city. When Aunt Esther and I visited the college, Tom was good enough to speak up just as we passed through the arch in the tower where he lives, by which they get into the college square. He said it was twelve o'clock, and we had to stop and hear him talk in that mighty, melodious tone. Another of the brothers is at Exeter, in the cathedral there, and so is called Tom of Exeter. Another, Tom of Lincoln, is in the cathedral of Lincoln. I must tell you what a writer, named Southey, wrote about this big fellow, when he went to make him a visit, some time ago. He says:

"We ascended one of the towers to see Great Tom, the largest bell in England. At first it disappointed me, but this disappointment soon wore off, and we became satisfied that it was as great a thing as it is said to be. A tall man might stand in it upright; the mouth measures one and twenty English feet in circumference, and it would be a large tree of which the girth would equal the size of the middle. The hours are struck upon it with a hammer."

On two days in the year they used to ring it by swinging it. One of these was Whitsunday, the other the day on which the judges come to Lincoln to hold the court. It was cracked a few years ago, and has never been used since. Around the bell runs this inscription:

"The Holy Ghost, proceeding from the Father and the Son, sweetly soundeth to salvation. Anno Domini, 3 December, 1610, in the 8th year of King James, of England, 44th of Scotland."

Do any of you ask why they gave these bells the name of "Tom?" It is probably because the boom of a great bell sounds so much like the word "Tom!" Tom Growler, however, got his first name of Edward in another way. As long ago as when he was a young fellow, it was customary in England, as it still is in some other countries, to *christen* bells, just in the same way as some folks now christen babies. That is, the priest would sprinkle the bell, "baptize" it as they called it,—and give it a name. Tom was "baptized" that way, and the name they first gave him was Edward. England was a Catholic country at that time.

When it became Protestant, people did not baptize bells any more; and as they did not think this bell I speak of was to be called Edward just because the priest named him so, and as he seemed always to be telling the world that his name was "*Tom!*" they finally decided that his name should be Tom, and Tom it is.

Now, I do not know whether all this will interest you much; but it will at least describe to you some of the curious things one meets with in old countries, and some of the curious ways of people there. Then, notice the inscription on the big bell at Lincoln, and that will give you something good to think about: "The Holy Ghost, proceeding from the Father and the Son, sweetly soundeth to salvation." Let us think of that, dear boys and girls, every time we hear the church bells ring.

UNCLE JOHN.

LETTER SEVENTEENTH.

HUMMING-BIRD CORNER.

Dear Boys and Girls:

YOU know, of course, what a museum is. Now the British Museum, in London, is one of the most wonderful in the world. Among the millions of curious things which it contains are collections of stuffed animals and birds. They are from almost every country under the sun; many of them strange looking creatures; many of them marvelously beautiful. One corner in the part devoted to birds I call "humming-bird corner." There is a large case there, containing hundreds of these beautiful creatures; some of them as large as a small sparrow, some of them no bigger than a bean. I used to always stop at this corner in passing through, and have another good look at the humming-birds.

One reason why I loved to look at them so, was that they gave me some pleasant things to think about. Among them was this — that evidently God has taken just as much pains with his little creatures as with his great creatures. Near by the place where the humming-birds are is another where they keep the eagles. You know what magnificent birds these are. The eagle is as much a king among birds as the lion among beasts. Here I saw them, great bold-eyed, strong-winged creatures, with talons, or claws, in which, while living, they could have taken up a child and carried him away through the air. There were eagles from the Alps, from the Himalayas, from the Andes, from the Rocky Mountains, some of them with wings, which, when stretched out, must have measured five or six feet across. It seemed to me, however, that in making the humming-birds, God had taken more pains, if I may speak that way, than in making the eagle;—certainly not less. In fact, the least of the little birds seemed most beautiful and most perfect, if possible, of all. Some tiny creatures, scarcely bigger than the end of my little finger, seemed the most beautiful things I ever saw;—their form was so perfect, their feathers were so delicate, their colors so brilliant.

Now, when one is a stranger in a great city like London, where there are three millions of people, scarcely a dozen of whom know anything of him, or care the least thing in the world about him, he is apt to feel very insignificant. Among these millions, too, there are a great many of vastly greater importance than himself. There is the Queen, there are princes and princesses, there are ministers, and dukes, and lords, and other great men who have in charge great affairs that concern not only the nation, but the world. One in such circumstances is tempted to say: "God will notice these great people, of course. If they need his help and care, doubtless he will give it to them, especially since they have such important things to look after. But how do I know that he cares anything for me?"

Then, in going along the street, perhaps one sees a little boy or girl looking utterly friendless and homeless, ragged, dirty, pale with hunger, with such a sorrowful face! One may feel as he goes by, "There is a child that has nobody to care for him. Nobody cares whether he lives or dies. Nobody cares whether or not he has any place to sleep in this wet, chilly night, or even a crust for his supper. Nobody cares whether his soul is saved or lost. What a poor, little waif! Just like some faded leaf carried along by the current of a great river."

Or perhaps some little child says, "I don't think God notices little children much, or cares very much about them. He hears grown-up people when they pray, especially if they are persons who have great and difficult things to do, or great troubles to bear; but I don't know if he will pay any attention to me if I do pray to him."

Now, the humming-birds taught me a lesson about these things. There is nothing too little to be important in God's eyes. He is just as particular in making little things as in making big things; just as careful with the tiny little humming-bird's bill, that is to have nothing greater to do than suck honey from a flower, as he is with the eagle's beak, that will tear the flesh of mighty beasts — paints as carefully and skillfully its diminutive wing, as he does the gaudy plumage of the peacock. Then I remembered these words: "Take heed that ye offend not one of these little ones, *for I say unto you that in heaven their angels do always behold the face of my Father which is in heaven.*" This is the only place in the Bible where such a wonderful thing is said, and it is said of the *little ones*. So I have learned to say, "Lord, let me be a little one; no matter *how* little; no matter how much lost in the world's mighty throng; no matter how poor and insignificant. *Thou* wilt not lose sight of me, but will love me all the more that I am a little one."

I think that God teaches the little ones in a very wonderful way, sometimes in the deepest and most difficult things of his kingdom. When little Jane, "the Young Cottager" of whom I wrote to you once before, was dying, her pastor, Mr. Richmond, asked her if she felt happy.

She said, "Yes."

"Do you think that when you die you will be *in* heaven?"

"Yes, very sure," she answered.

"What makes you think so?"

She pointed with her weak finger towards heaven, and then towards her own bosom, and replied, "Christ *there*, and Christ *here*."

It is seldom that even old and experienced Christians give a better reason for the hope that is in them.

Never let your unbelief make you think that God is not glad to hear you pray, or to do everything necessary for you; above all to prepare you, through his grace that is in his Son, Jesus Christ, for death and for heaven.

Uncle John.

LETTER EIGHTEENTH.

NEVERSINK HEIGHTS.

Dear Boys and Girls:

NOW that I am "home again," I must write you one more letter, and then say "good-bye." You have been very patient and good, if you have read all these that are here printed. If you have found in them something which it will be pleasant and profitable to you to remember, I shall be truly glad. Something, now, about our voyage home will finish my letters, and my book.

On the morning of the twelfth day after we sailed from Liverpool, in the good and beautiful ship "Wisconsin," as I was walking the deck in the after-part of the ship — that is near the stern — I heard some boys and girls cry out, "Come and see the land!" and saw them run with all their might the whole length of the vessel to its "forecastle" or prow. They did not say "Come!" to me, but I thought, nevertheless, that I should like to see the land too, and so I went. With my old eyes I could discover nothing at all but what I had seen for the twelve days back, that is, sea and sky, but taking my glass I made out, directly in front of the ship, far away on the western horizon, some blue heights, which seemed at first like a cloud, but which I soon perceived were the welcome land. The "forecastle" is where the "steerage passengers," or the emigrants, mostly stay, and they had crowded now to the extreme forward end of the ship, and were gazing across the waters at the same distant blue hills. They were principally Irish or Germans. This which was before them was their first view of what was to them a strange land. To me it was *home*, and it seemed wonderfully beautiful on that bright morning, seen across the blue waters, rippling under a balmy breeze, and shining in the rays of the blessed sun.

Turning back again, after a while, I met a gentleman who used to be a sea-captain, and had crossed the ocean, he told me, some two or three hundred times.

"Will you tell me," I asked him, "what land that is?"

"It is the Heights of Neversink," he said, "in New Jersey. Just there our ship will turn into the bay, and we shall then soon be at New York."

"Neversink Heights," I thought, "it is a good name." Some people, I believe, call them Navesink, and that may be their Indian name for aught I know, but I shall call them *Neversink*. And they never do sink. They are some of the "everlasting hills." Ships may sink out in the sea, in sight of them, but they "never sink." Generation after generation of those who live on or near them may sink into the grave, but they stand erect just the same. The storm raging onward from the sea tries to overthrow them, but it cannot. The winter strips their green woods of their beauty, but the summer clothes them again. The torrents that run down their sides seek to carry them away into the ocean; but the firm hills only smile at the feeble attempt. Till all the world's mountains sink, these will "never sink."

Now, dear children, are there any other "Heights of Neversink?" any which you yourselves may sometimes discover blue in the distance as you sail upon another sea, towards another city? Any which, perhaps, you may visit and climb? I think there are. The Heights of Truth are Heights of Neversink. The Heights of Divine Promise are Heights of Neversink. The Heights of Christian Hope are Heights of Neversink; and many a one, climbing to their summit, has seen the Celestial City, near at hand or far away, its spires glittering in that glory of the Lord which is its sun by day and its moon by night.

But there is another thing I must tell you. When I got my first view of Neversink Heights the ship was going directly towards them. If we had kept right on, without stopping, the sails full and the engine going, we should have been dashed upon the shore, and what had been so welcome, as we saw it out at sea, would have been our ruin. Suppose, now, a ship should be sailing there some dark and stormy night, with not a star to be seen, and nothing to show whether any land was near or not. The wind carries it forward with furious speed through the darkness, while the man on the lookout tries in vain to see if there is any danger ahead. There is danger there, is there not? Unless in some way those who sail the ship are warned, they will be driven upon the shore and wrecked and lost. To prevent such disasters as this a lighthouse is placed at Neversink Heights, just at the point where ships must turn to go up into the bay. And now, when the sailor comes near those Heights in the dark night, he sees the friendly beacon, and knows that up by way of the lighthouse is the safe passage into the harbor and on to the city.

Now, I think that the youngest of you can understand that we need to know not only *what* the truth is, but *where* it is, and how by means of it to find our way to the city of God. There are some, I am sorry to say, who go to wreck upon the truth itself. Does not the apostle speak of the Gospel as "the savour of death unto death" to some, while "the savour of life unto life" to others? God's Revealed Word is the Lighthouse. This shows us what the truth is, where it is, and makes us understand that he has planted these Neversink Heights here in this world, not for us to run our ships upon, but that they may point us the way to the Blessed Harbor and to the Celestial City. Does it not seem strange that any should despise the friendly light, sail on just as if there was no light there, and be "ground to powder" against that which was meant, not for their destruction, but for their salvation?

These are some of the things which Neversink Heights made me think about, and I thought I would just mention them to you because I want you all to love the Truth, and to so use the Truth that you may be saved. You are in sight of Neversink Heights every time you learn aright a lesson of God's blessed word; you have the Heights and the Lighthouse both. Don't let the man at the helm — that obstinate fellow whom we call Will — don't let him steer the good ship so as to wreck it *against* the Truth, but so as that the Truth may guide you and light you safe home to God. In other words, be willing — humbly, meekly willing — to confess every sin, and to trust in Jesus only, *only*, ONLY, for the pardon of them all.

And now, good-bye. It seems odd, does it not, to say "good-bye" just as I am coming home? But then, you see, even if I continue to be "Uncle John," I shall not be "Uncle John Upon his Travels" any more. I am almost sorry that I shall not. It has been nice to see so many interesting things, and it has made me very happy to tell you of some of them. But it does not answer to be running about and looking up pleasant sights all one's life, and so I come home to my work again. Good-bye, then. God bless and save every one of you. God raise you up many and many better friends than Uncle John has known how to be. Above all, may he himself be your friend, and nothing can be better than that.

UNCLE JOHN.

www.ingramcontent.com/pod-product-compliance
Lightning Source LLC
Chambersburg PA
CBHW032225230426
43666CB00033B/1595